Truth in a Nutshell

Small bites of Bible wisdom for daily nourishment

John Mollitt

Onwards and Upwards Publishers

Berkeley House, 11 Nightingale Crescent, Leatherhead,
Surrey, KT24 6PD.

www.onwardsandupwards.org

Printed in the UK by 4edge Limited.

ISBN: 978-1-910197-76-9
Typeface: Sabon LT
Graphic design: LM Graphic Design

About the Author

John Mollitt was born in the Lune Valley, near to Lancaster. Having worked in banking and the Civil Service, he became Pastor of Ingleton Evangelical Church, North Yorkshire in 1979. He retired in 2009 and is now engaged in an itinerant preaching ministry.

John is married to Pat and has three children and five grandchildren. He enjoys watching sport, playing chess and has a nostalgic interest in steam railways.

Endorsements

"In his book 'The Craft of the Sermon' the Methodist preacher W.E. Sangster spoke of the importance of illustrations and anecdotes. He said they served as 'windows' which let light in on the truth we are presenting. In his teaching the Lord Jesus often did this.

On many occasions I have felt that some preachers have been guilty of preaching the truth without the practical application to the lives and circumstances of those to whom they minister. It hasn't always been 'grounded truth'.

John Mollitt's many years of pastoral ministry have given him the opportunity to preach and to apply the truth not only to his own congregation in Ingleton but also to a wider audience.

These anecdotes collected over a period of time are both comforting and challenging – and to Christians and non-Christians alike.

Each one is solidly based on Scripture but applied simply to everyday situations which we must all face. They will do you good."

Derek Cleave
Evangelist, Author and Chaplain

"This is a very personal and precious book, containing nuggets of pure gold. The material will be helpful to Christians, challenging to unbelievers, a real comfort and blessing to struggling Christians and a very helpful resource for preachers!"

Peter Parkinson
Co-founder, Caring for Life[1]

---

[1] Caring for Life (CFL) is a Christian charity based in Leeds. Established in 1987, CFL has shown the love of Jesus in practical ways to vulnerable and homeless men and women for over twenty-five years

Contents

8

Foreword by Roger Carswell

I love my books. When travelling, and away from my 'library', I miss them. Books are for reading and for reference, and it is those that are useful for both that I enjoy most. I have biographies galore, books of sermons, some history, others on a variety of themes, numerous commentaries, dictionaries, and then my favourites: collections of quotations, illustrations and anecdotes. To me they are priceless. I have scoured new and second hand bookshops to secure the variety that I dip into constantly. If my mind is dull and needs sharpening, these volumes never disappoint; if my sermons appear heavy, I'll find something in these resources to lighten the load; and if I just need something to keep the attention of the people with whom I am communicating, either one to one or to a crowd, there is salt in these books to savour the conversation or the proclamation. Even just one good, useful anecdote in a whole volume makes the book worth the price!

John Mollitt has lived a life which I find deeply challenging. Now he has passed on to us, not an autobiography, which would have been great in itself, but an accessible and fascinating distillation of experiences and insights which cannot help but benefit the individual reader and the preacher alike. Anything which drives home Bible truths is to be commended. 'Truth in a Nutshell' fits the bill. It may be a little quirky, but the acknowledging smiles on your face, then your desire to pass on what you have just read, and the biblical truths impressed on your mind, will make you glad that you dipped into insights from the life of a faithful man of God who loves His Saviour, and so admirably serves His Lord. This book is packed with gems which, if imbibed and passed on, will make you all the more interesting to be with!

Roger Carswell
Evangelist and Author

ADOPTION

ROMANS 8:15-17; GALATIANS 4:4-7

My wife and I became foster parents with Lancashire Social Services in 1985. Initially, we cared for two babies; one we picked up from hospital when he was five days old, and the other came to us as a six-month-old baby. Christopher stayed with us for five weeks, and Michelle for six months. We were sad when the time came for them to move on.

In November 1987, we were asked to foster a multi-handicapped baby boy. Aaron came to us when he was ten weeks old and we fostered him for the next sixteen years. Friday 2nd April 2004 was a momentous day – it was the day Aaron stopped being fostered and was adopted into our family. He became a Mollitt, and on that day everything changed. He took our name and our address. He became our child and the inheritor – for what it is worth – of all that we possess. And he entered into a relationship that is now permanent and not temporary.

As believers we have been adopted – not fostered – into the family of God. It is a permanent arrangement, not temporary.

> *God sent his Son ... that we might receive adoption to sonship.*
>
> Galatians 4:4-5

11

How amazing! By nature we are the children of the devil but, through grace, God has adopted us into His family. We needed a Father, but God did not need any more sons because He already had a Son who was perfect, a Son who was the apple of His eye. How amazing that He should adopt us and grant us a change of name, a change of address, a change of status. We are now called Christians; heaven is our home; and as the children of God, we are joint heirs with Jesus and the possessors of innumerable riches.

Realise afresh the wonder of your adoption!

ASCENSION OF JESUS

MARK 16:19

In 1974, Morecambe beat Dartford in the FA Trophy Final at Wembley Stadium. They defeated the opposition by two goals to one. I was in Morecambe when the players arrived back in the resort. They rode on an open top bus, displaying the trophy, and as they did so, thousands sang, applauded and cheered. They welcomed home their conquering heroes.

It is a mundane illustration, but a slight insight into what happened on Ascension Day. On Easter Day, Jesus triumphed. He rose victorious over sin, death, Satan and hell. He defeated the enemy. That was Easter Day – but forty days later, Jesus returned home. He ascended and the whole of heaven – angels, archangels, cherubims, seraphims and thousands of His saints – turned out to acknowledge and to acclaim His triumph.

> *From the fight returned victorious.*
> *Every knee to Him shall bow.*[2]

---

[2] From the hymn 'Look, Ye Saints, The Sight Is Glorious'

ATHEISM

PSALM 14:1; ROMANS 8:7

'When I was a child, I was taught about God, Father Christmas and the Tooth Fairy. I soon realised that two of these were kidology, made up by my parents. Soon afterwards, I came to the same conclusion about the Tooth Fairy.'

It is sad, but so read a letter in a recent national newspaper. Hard, cynical atheism; and yet I can never understand why atheists are so angry and cynical about Someone who, they say, does not exist. I never feel that way about Father Christmas or the Tooth Fairy!

BACKSLIDING

JEREMIAH 3:22

One Saturday night, I was with a group who were handing out tracts[3], when a boisterous group of men emerged from a pub. Many of them were worse for drink and they began to mock and to blaspheme.

As they made their way to the next pub, one of the group stayed behind. He confessed there had been a time when he had trusted Jesus and he did not want to be identified with his friends in mocking us and in blaspheming Jesus.

As I talked with the man, I had every reason to believe he was a backslider, and our conversation confirmed two things about backsliding:

- the backslider is never a happy man;
- backsliding always takes you further than you want to go.

The man was OK whilst he was drinking with his friends, but distressed when their drinking turned to abuse and blasphemy.

---

[3] leaflets about Christianity

BAPTISM

When my children were young, sometimes they would protest if they had to be bathed in the same water. 'I am not going in that. He/she has been in it. I want some clean water.'

Jesus was baptised in the River Jordan and it was 'dirty' because in its waters sinners had confessed a multitude of sins. And yet Jesus was baptised in that same river because he wished to identify Himself with sinful men and women.

BIBLE (I)

ISAIAH 40:8

When I was thirteen, I received an Encyclopaedia of Science for Christmas. The sciences were never my strong subjects and so the encyclopaedia was of great help as I prepared for GCEs in Chemistry and Physics. However, it was not much help to my children when they took their exams in the 1990s, and in the future it will be of even less help to my grandchildren. Why? Much of the information is now out of date or irrelevant.

There is only one Book which never grows old, is never out of date and is always relevant. That Book is the Bible. How sad that so many never learn from its pages.

BIBLE (II)

The Bible should never be used as a horoscope – by which I mean we should never just pick a verse out and use it as a motto for that day. And yet, there have been times when the verse for the day on my Scriptural calendar has remarkably addressed the situation.

One day, a young woman was in our home in deep distress because it seemed that she and her husband would never have the child for which they longed. My wife and I spoke with her, but our words brought her little comfort.

I went up to my study and the text on the calendar that day was the words of Eli spoken to Hannah when she was in great distress because of her childlessness:

> *'Go in peace, and may the God of Israel grant you what you have asked of him.'*
>
> 1 Samuel 1:17

I gained an inner certainty that the young woman would conceive and I told her so. Twelve months later she joyfully shared the news that she was pregnant.

On another occasion, a man from a very difficult background was converted but I was anxious about him. I saw the difficulties that he would now experience in his home and at work, and I wondered how he would fare. The text on my calendar that morning? Romans 14:4:

*Indeed, he will be made to stand, for God is able
to make him stand.*

Over thirty years later, he is still progressing heavenward.

BIBLE (III)

HEBREWS 4:12

In the 1970s, I did open air work in Blackpool with Pastor John Pennington. John was a real character, but even as an elderly man he never lost his zeal and fervour.

One night, as he preached to a queue outside a nightclub, a quietness came over the crowd. John paused and quietly said, 'I see the cap has fit and I've not even measured your head.' This is the power of the Word as it convicts and challenges.

A man in Ingleton once accused me of telling a visiting preacher all about him. I had done no such thing. It was God who knew all about Him and through His Word, He was convicting and challenging that man.

Bible (IV)

There are two Ingletons – Ingleton (North Yorkshire) where I live and Ingleton (County Durham). On one occasion, I received a phone call from a man wishing to get married at the village church in Ingleton. The phone call was most confusing and I could not make any sense of it, until I realised that the person had got the wrong Ingleton. It was the Ingleton church in County Durham he wanted, not the one in North Yorkshire.

There were two Bethlehems in Israel in Bible times, and that is why Micah, in his prophecy, specified Bethlehem Ephrata. There is nothing vague or ambiguous about biblical prophecy – what is foretold has and always will come to pass, right down to the smallest detail.

> *For prophecy never had its origin in the human will, but prophets, though human, spoke from God as they were carried along by the Holy Spirit.*
>
> 2 Peter 1:21

21

BIBLE (V)

COLOSSIANS 3:16

I once went with my brother to preach at the harvest thanksgiving services in a Yorkshire Dales village. We took the afternoon service and were told where we would be having tea prior to the evening service.

When we arrived at the house, the lady said, 'I am sure you don't want to come inside yet, on such a beautiful afternoon. Go for a drive and come back at 5pm.' We did as suggested, and when we got back a most acceptable tea was set before us. But instead of talking with us, the lady sat in her chair and watched a programme on television. We got the feeling that we were not altogether wanted and we certainly did not feel at home.

Does the Word of God feel at home in our hearts? Not if we ignore or doubt it. Not if we resent or resist it. But if we welcome and obey the Word, even when we are humbled and rebuked by it, then the Word of God will feel at home in our hearts.

BIRTH OF JESUS (I)

LUKE 1:26-33

My R.E. teacher at school rejected the Virgin Birth because he said it meant that Jesus would be different from us. But surely that is the message of the New Testament, for what hope would there be for anyone if Jesus was just the same as you and I?

'Those who deny that Jesus was without human father must explain how He was without human failure.'

John Blanchard

BIRTH OF JESUS (II)

LUKE 2:7; JOHN 1:10-11

I was a small boy when one August we went to spend a few days in Colwyn Bay. We had not booked in advance – we intended just having bed and breakfast for three or four days. But it was the 1950s, when British seaside resorts were booming, and so we got the same response at house after house: 'Sorry, no room, no vacancies. We are full.'

It was getting towards dusk, and we were preparing to spend the night in the waiting room at Colwyn Bay railway station, when my father knocked on one more door. Thankfully, the lady took pity on us and somehow managed to accommodate us under her roof.

A not dissimilar situation faced Mary and Joseph when Jesus was about to be born. Bethlehem was full. No rooms were available. There was not even a railway station. No, all they could find was a stable attached to an inn, and it was there that Jesus was born.

Sadly, what was true of Bethlehem is increasingly true of many in Britain today. People are so busy, with so many demands upon them, that they can find no room for Jesus. How tragic it is – no room for the King of Kings, the Lord of Lords.

Room for pleasure, room for business,
But for Christ the Crucified,
Not a place that He can enter,
In the heart for which He died?[4]

---

[4] From the hymn 'Have You Any Room For Jesus?'
(Anonymous; adapted by Daniel W. Whittle)

BIRTH OF JESUS (III)

MATTHEW 1:21; 1 TIMOTHY 1:15

I once had a birthday which I will never forget – because everyone else did! I woke early that morning and my wife was very chatty but no mention was made of my birthday. After a while, I sang, 'Happy Birthday to me. Happy Birthday to me. Happy Birthday, dear John. Happy Birthday to me.'

Pat was apologetic, but had no need to be because only the previous evening she had been diagnosed with a potentially serious medical condition. So it was understandable that this dominated her thoughts.

Just before 8am, the telephone rang and I could see that it was my daughter, Joanna. Joanna never forgets a birthday. I picked the phone up and Joanna said, 'How is Mum?'

'Do you want a word with her?' I said, and mother and daughter proceeded to talk for the next ten minutes.

The phone was put down and again I sang, 'Happy birthday to me. Happy birthday to me. Happy birthday, dear John. Happy birthday to me.'

Early that evening, the telephone rang and it was my son, Andrew. This is amazing, I thought, he never ever remembers a birthday.

'Hello, Andrew,' I said.

'Hi, Dad,' he responded, 'do you have my MOT certificate?'

We chatted for a few minutes but no mention was made of my birthday, and again I sang, 'Happy birthday to me. Happy birthday to me. Happy birthday, dear John, Happy birthday to me.'

My birthday had been forgotten, but in truth, I was not too concerned – I have reached an age when I perhaps prefer them to be forgotten, rather than be remembered. Far more serious is the fact that, increasingly, the birth of Jesus is being forgotten. More and more Christmas songs are secular and it is not easy now to find a Christmas card which has any reference to His birth. Christmas is celebrated as Xmas or a Winter Festival, and the birth, the Incarnation of Jesus, is all but ignored.

This is serious because when His birth is forgotten, so too is the purpose of His birth. 'Christ Jesus came into the world to save sinners…' Not just at Christmas but every day, let us remember a unique Person who came for a unique purpose.

BIRTH OF JESUS (IV)

MATTHEW 1:23

Pat enjoys making birthday cards, Christmas cards, cards for all occasions – and the proceeds go to support Christian charities. Finding it difficult to buy any Christmas cards with a nativity theme, Pat decided to make her own. On each card she put the words 'Immanuel – God with us'. On Christmas Eve, a card came through the post addressed to 'John, Pat, Aaron and Immanuel'. The sender must have thought there had been an addition to our family!

We can call a child 'Immanuel' but the only true Immanuel is Jesus – the Son of God. And yet, through faith in Him, God can be with us, just as He was with Mary and Joseph, two thousand years ago. The God who is 'far above us' can be 'with us' in the person of Jesus Christ.

BIRTH OF JESUS (V)

LUKE 2:10-11; 2 CORINTHIANS 9:15

In the weeks leading up to Christmas, Pat was speaking to the wife of the retired minister who had married us. 'If you ever want to get John a book on penal substitution,' the woman said, 'you must buy "Pierced for our Transgressions". My husband says it is excellent.'

Taking her advice, Pat duly ordered the book and presented it to me on Christmas morning. I was immediately faced with a moral dilemma: did I pretend to be thrilled or did I tell the truth? You see, two years earlier, I had given that minister a copy of 'Pierced for our Transgressions'. Much thought had gone into the buying of the book but, unfortunately, I had already read it.

Not all gifts we give or receive at Christmas are appropriate but God's gift of His Son is appropriate for all. Rich or poor, educated or uneducated, young or old, we all need a Saviour, and Jesus Christ is the Saviour we need.

The angel said, 'Behold I bring you good tidings of great joy which will be to *all* people. For there is born to you this day in the city of David a Saviour who is Christ the Lord.'

BLOOD OF CHRIST

ISAIAH 1:18, 64:6; 1 JOHN 1:7; REVELATION 7:13-14

I've had a beard since the mid-1970s, so shaving is not an everyday occurrence. But from time to time I do shave, and on one occasion I carelessly gashed my neck. The cut was quite deep and I had to change my shirt because it was stained with blood. Blood is something not easy to remove.

And yet it is only blood – the blood of Jesus Christ – which can wash and cleanse me from the dirt and filth of my sin. Amazing, but true. The question asked in Revelation 7, 'Who are these arrayed in white robes...?' is met with the answer, 'These are the ones who ... washed their robes and made them white in the blood of the Lamb.' (NKJV) The blood of Christ applied to 'filthy rags' results in 'white robes'.

CARE AND COMPASSION

MATTHEW 10:29-31

We were enjoying a family holiday in Derbyshire with our children and grandchildren. But the joy was broken on the fifth morning when my daughter Joanna announced, 'We will have to go back to Leeds.' Why? Was someone ill? Had their house been burgled? No – they had forgotten to feed the goldfish!

This news was met with incredulity by most of the party, and it was suggested that Joanna could always buy some more goldfish if the fish were floating when she got back from holiday.

Joanna was not amused, and after breakfast, her husband, Al, was dispatched on a 180-mile round journey to 'rescue the perishing'. We waited with bated breath, but eventually the phone call came, to tell us that the fish were still alive and swimming. My hope of a fish and chip supper had disappeared!

Joanna's care and concern for the goldfish was amusing, but God's care and concern for His children is truly amazing.

CHRISTIAN LIFE (I)

GENESIS 5:21-24

As a young boy, my grandparents came every Wednesday to see us. They did not live far away but it took two bus journeys to get to us. When they got off the bus in Morecambe, they then had a half-mile walk to our home.

Many times we thought that Grandad had come on his own because he would come round the corner and there was no sight of Grandma. But then, supported by her stick, Grandma would appear – arriving at our house some minutes after Grandad. They had been married for over sixty years but their walk was not as close as one might have desired.

You may have been walking with the Lord for a few or for many years, but is your walk with Him as close as it might be? Surely, we all need to pray, 'O for a closer walk with God.' Enoch had the wonderful testimony that he 'walked with God'.

Christian Life (II)

2 Corinthians 8:9

When our son Andrew was born, we opened a building society account in his name. When he was sixteen, we handed the book over to him and there was a balance of just over £200.

Andrew put the book to the back of a drawer and forgot all about it, until he found it again some ten years later. He went into the local office of the building society to have the book brought up to date, and to his amazement came out with a balance of almost £3,000. In the intervening years the building society had become a bank and its customers had benefitted from a windfall payment. Andrew was far richer than he had ever imagined himself to be.

I used to visit an elderly lady who, though she lived in a detached bungalow, was far from wealthy. She was on welfare benefits and kept selling items of furniture in order to help with household expenses. One afternoon, she said she had some money which she wanted me to count, and she produced three envelopes from a cabinet. I was astounded to discover £3,000 in the first envelope, £4,000 in the second envelope, and in the third envelope – £5,000.

On expressing my surprise, the lady told me that the money was not hers as it belonged to her sister. This might have once been the case, but as her sister had died some years previously, the money was now hers. She was living in poverty because she had no idea just how rich she was.

I fear that is often true of believers. How rich we are in Christ – our sins are forgiven, we are reconciled to God, we are indwelt by His Spirit, and we have the promise of an eternal home in heaven. We are heirs of God, joint-heirs with Christ. How rich we are, and yet how often we walk in this world as though we are spiritual paupers.

CHRISTIAN LIFE (III)

MARK 8:22-25; 1 CORINTHIANS 13:12

Due to cataracts, my grandmother was blind. But at the age of eighty-five she went into hospital and a cataract was removed from one eye. What a difference. Her sight was far from being perfect, but the blindness had been taken away. Now she could see.

We are born into this world spiritually blind and in darkness, but through the miracle of regeneration our eyes are opened and we begin to see spiritual truth. Our sight will not be perfect until we reach heaven, but how thankful we should be that our blindness has been taken away.

As a small boy, I was sometimes with my mother when she was buying a new hat, a new coat or a new dress. I can remember the sales assistant taking the article to the shop window or even outside. Why? In the relative darkness of the store, you could not be sure of the colour. The colour only became clear in the daylight, in the sunshine.

The same is true of spiritual things. We are still in the dark, in the shadows, but when the Son shines in all His glory, then 'we shall see and hear and know, all we desired and wished below'[5].

---

[5] From the hymn 'Sweet is the Work, My God, My King' by Isaac Watts (1674-1748)

CHRISTIAN LIFE (IV)

ACTS 17:10-11; MARK 8:14-21; MATTHEW 18:1-6

The preacher had taught about the meeting of Paul and King Agrippa. As they walked home from the service, my mother asked my brother what the preacher had been speaking about. His answer was quite definite: 'Paul and a tin of kippers.'

Children don't always get it right, but neither do we. Everything must be tested by the Word of God.

We were in the car with our grandson one day, when a police car raced by with lights flashing and siren sounding.

'O dear,' said my wife, Pat, 'someone must have had an accident.'

With childlike innocence, the three-year-old asked, 'Why – have they wet their pants?'

The disciples did not always understand what Jesus meant and neither do we, but let us keep our childlike trust in Him.

CHRISTIAN LIFE (V)

1 CORINTHIANS 6:9-11; ISAIAH 61:10; JAMES 1:27;
1 JOHN 1:9

When Joanna was a young girl and going to a party, Pat would wash her and put a clean dress on her. Pat would then say to Joanna, 'Don't get dirty, keep yourself clean. I've got you ready for the party.'

Inevitably, sometimes Joanna got dirty again!

As believers, we are washed in the blood of Jesus, we are clothed in the garment of salvation, we are dressed for heaven. How important it is that we keep ourselves pure and do not become soiled by the dirt and filth of this world.

However, if we do become tainted, fresh cleansing is always available. Thank you, Lord!

CHRISTIAN LIFE (VI)

HEBREWS 12:2

For a number of years, I started the races at the sports day at the junior school in Ingleton. The pre-school race was always the most amusing. A three or four year old would be running well until they were distracted by the sight of Mum and Dad in the crowd. They would then stop or stumble and be overtaken by those whose eyes were still on the finishing tape.

Sadly, believers sometimes stagger and stumble because they become distracted. Instead of keeping their eyes 'fixed on Jesus', they look to their brothers and sisters in Christ. If these fail them, they then become discouraged and disillusioned.

The only one who is never going to let us down is Jesus.

CHRISTIAN LIFE (VII)

HEBREWS 12:1-2

Two or three times a year, as youngsters, we would put money in the slot and stand on one of those weighing machines which were a feature of many shops in the 1950s and 1960s. Being twins, there was never much difference in weight between me and my brother. So one day it was a surprise to notice that Jim was several pounds heavier than me. The mystery was soon solved when we discovered that Jim had got on the scales with a shopping bag in his right hand!

Excess weight is not good for us either physically or spiritually. When we are first converted, we all come with 'baggage' – hurts, problems, attitudes from the past. But as we are sanctified by the Truth, as we grow in grace, so these things are dealt with and we are not as 'weighed' down by them as once we were.

For by one sacrifice he has made perfect for ever those who are being made holy.

Hebrews 10:14

CHRISTIAN SERVICE (I)

2 CORINTHIANS 6:1

One morning a young woman came into the Job Centre where I worked and excitedly told me that she had got work as a domestic servant. Why was she so thrilled? Well, the post was at Buckingham Palace! She was to work for the monarch.

When in his eighties, my grandfather would walk two miles to the village chapel every Saturday night. When he got there, he did two things. He wound the clock and he got the hymnbooks out for the Sunday School. Menial tasks, but the important thing was not so much the task, it was the One for whom the task was being done. He was working for the King of Kings. He was in the employment of the Sovereign and it was that which made all the difference.

CHRISTIAN SERVICE (II)

JOHN 14:6; 2 CORINTHIANS 12:9-10

I was travelling down the M62 when I saw a huge text displayed in a field. It proclaimed, 'Jesus said: "I am the *way*, the *truth* and the *life*. No one comes to the Father except through Me."' It thrilled my heart to think of the thousands who every day must see those words.

But why is it there? Well, yes, some individual or group has arranged for the text to be displayed, but that is only the secondary reason. That text is there because Thomas said, 'Lord, we don't know where You are going, so how can we know the way?' (John 14:5). And it was in response to that question asked by Thomas, in unbelief and weakness, that Jesus gave the answer, through which multitudes have come to saving faith.

How reassuring to know that the Lord can take even my doubts and weaknesses and use them for His glory.

CHRISTIAN SERVICE (III)

MATTHEW 24:45-51

At school, there were occasions when a teacher had to leave the classroom. Knowing this, he would leave us work to do while he was away – perhaps a book to read or an essay to write. There was always lots of work to do while the teacher was out, but what I often noticed was this: when the teacher was away, we were never as keen or as enthusiastic as we were when the teacher was present. There was plenty of work to do, but without the teacher we somehow lost the motivation, the incentive, to do it.

Jesus knew this would be a temptation facing his followers in every generation once He had returned to heaven – when the cat is away, the mice will play. This is why, again and again, Jesus urged His disciples to be diligent and industrious in the time between His Ascension and His Second Coming.

Are we making the most of every opportunity (Colossians 4:5) or just coasting till He comes?

CHRISTIAN SERVICE (IV)

MARK 6:34-44; EPHESIANS 2:8-10; JAMES 1:27

As a child and as an unconverted teenager, I heard my grandfather preach and pray. And yet, it was something else which made an impact on me.

Well into his eighties, he spent two or three afternoons a week visiting the sick and those in need. On Wednesdays, when he visited us in Morecambe, he would catch the bus to Heysham after lunch. Here he called on an aged aunt, before walking the three miles back to our home. On route he visited sick and housebound people whom he knew in Morecambe.

At a quarter past five, the door would open and Grandad had returned – having been a signalman on the railway, you could set your watch by him. We would then sit round the fireside whilst he updated us on all the people he had visited.

According to the New Testament, this is authentic Christianity, demonstrated by the Lord Himself. Jesus not only preached to the multitudes but had compassion on them and fed them.

CHRISTIAN SERVICE (V)

JOHN 4:36; 1 CORINTHIANS 15:58

One Monday morning, a group of workmen came into the Department of Employment office in Morecambe. They had been working for a sub-contractor on a building site but when they went to pick up their wages on the Friday, they discovered he had disappeared. They had worked all week for nothing.

That will never be true of anyone who has worked for Jesus, who has faithfully toiled in the harvest fields of the kingdom. Jesus promises we will receive our 'wages', whilst Paul assures us that our work for the Lord will never be 'in vain'.

What an incentive to be busy and active in the service of Jesus.

CHRISTIAN SERVICE (VI)

2 SAMUEL 24:24

I had taken the midweek Bible Study and afterwards the church treasurer thanked me and placed an envelope in my hand. On arriving home, I opened the envelope, only to discover it was empty. There was nothing in it. Pat joked, 'That is what they must have thought of your Bible Study.' It was of course a mistake and a few weeks later an embarrassed treasurer was on the phone, as he tried to balance his accounts for the month.

There is a serious point to this humorous incident. Does our worship, our giving, our service cost us anything or are we just content to offer to the Lord that which makes no demands upon us?

CHURCH (I)

JOHN 4:19-24

The church building in which I pastored for thirty years had previously been a Co-op shop and then a car showroom. It was a wonderful testimony to God's faithfulness that a small group of believers had been able to purchase the property. And yet I know there were those in the village who would never come to any of our services because, in their eyes, we were not a 'proper' church.

In contrast, when we read the words of Jesus in John 4 we see that the important thing is not *where* we worship, but rather *whom* and *how* we worship.

May we not be so preoccupied with the place that we fail to truly worship the Person.

CHURCH (II)

As a teenager, I was a member of Lancaster Chess Club for several years. Our secretary was a retired college lecturer, but besides being our secretary he was also the club captain and our best player.

One evening we were returning from a tournament where the team had been beaten and unusually Mr Turner had also lost his match. As we travelled he said, 'I don't wish to make excuses but it isn't conducive to good chess when someone says, "Mr Turner, the kettle is boiling."' The poor man was not only our secretary, captain and best player – he was expected to brew the tea as well.

Are there believers in churches 'weary in well doing' because they are overworked – having to do everything – whilst others 'sit at ease in Zion', unwilling to bear any responsibility? How the Church of Jesus Christ needs men and women today who are 'steadfast, immovable, always abounding in the work of the Lord...' (1 Corinthians 15:58, NKJV).

CHURCH (III)

I was having difficulties with a man in the church, so I shared my problem with a retired minister. 'John, you must remember,' the minister said, 'the Lord has some in His family that we perhaps would not want in ours.' A very helpful comment.

However difficult a believer might be, they have been chosen by God, saved by Christ and indwelt by the Holy Spirit. He or she is our brother or sister in Christ and we must love and treat them as such.

CHURCH (IV)

EPHESIANS 5:25B-27

I knew I must be getting older when, for my birthday, my family bought me a one-thousand-piece jigsaw. It was entitled 'Grandad's Attic', and on the box there was a heart-warming picture of a grandfather and grandson playing with a train set in the attic.

But very often I struggled with the jigsaw. I could not get the pieces to fit together, and sometimes I looked with incredulity at the picture on the box. What I had before me bore no resemblance to what was on the box.

In the Bible – on the box – it says that the Church of Christ will become 'a radiant church, without stain or wrinkle or any other blemish, but holy and blameless' (Ephesians 5:27). But when I see the Church and my own heart, I sometimes wonder, 'Is it possible?' What I now see is not what is on the box. But, praise God, His Word will be fulfilled. His Church will be glorious. His people will be perfect.

Be assured – what is on the box will come to pass.

CREATION

I was asked to speak at a Harvest Supper and I got Pat to bake an apple pie for me. At the supper, I explained that the apple pie was a most amazing pie because it had made itself. The ingredients had come together to form the pastry, the apples had fallen into the pastry, the pastry had jumped into the oven and then, after half an hour, the pie had emerged brown, cooked and ready to eat... The people looked at me as though I was talking nonsense – and of course I was. Behind the apple pie, there was a baker, a person – my wife.

Is it not astounding that people can think this universe – so majestic, so beautiful, so intricate, so ordered – just happened? No Creator – there was just a 'big bang' and something came out of nothing. Surely, that is far more incredible than an apple pie making itself, and yet that is what multitudes have been taught and believe.

CROSS (I)

MATTHEW 27:46; HEBREWS 9:22

Aaron, our son, was in Manchester Children's Hospital for major surgery. We were understandably anxious as we accompanied him to the doors of the operating theatre. Why would loving parents ever subject their son to the pain of the surgeon's knife? There is only one explanation. It was necessary.

Why did God subject His Son – the apple of His eye – to the pain and humiliation of the cross? There is only one explanation. It was necessary.

> *There was no other good enough*
> *To pay the price of sin;*
> *He only could unlock the gate*
> *Of heaven, and let us in.*[6]

---

[6] From the hymn 'There is a Green Hill Far Away' by Cecil Frances Alexander

CROSS (II)

Driving our four-year-old granddaughter back to her home, we passed a village church with a cross outside. 'Nana,' she said, 'that is where God died.'

Elodie could not possibly understand the profundity of what she was saying. But did God die at Calvary? Was Charles Wesley right: 'Amazing love! How can it be that Thou, my God, shouldst die for me?' Did God die at Calvary?

It is a theological issue beyond our comprehending and perhaps the best we can say is this. Jesus was the God/Man and He never ceased to be God, even when hanging on the cross. But Jesus had to die as a man because He was dying as our substitute, and it is impossible for God to die. In the words of John Owen, 'He suffered not as God but He who suffered was God.'

How thankful we should be that, through the cross, Jesus – the God/Man – has reconciled man to God and God to man.

CROSS (III)

GALATIANS 3:13

Visiting a shopping mall, we decided to have a coffee at a restaurant on the first floor. Having Aaron with us meant Pat having to use the lift.

Unfortunately, half-way up the lift stopped, and Pat and Aaron were suspended between the two floors. Not a desirable but rather a disturbing situation in which to find oneself.

When Jesus died upon the cross, He was suspended between earth and heaven, and that was significant. Earth did not want Jesus, because in the eyes of men He was a criminal; and heaven did not want Him because Jesus was bearing our sin. Rejected by earth and by heaven – how great was His suffering?

> *We may not know, we cannot tell,*
> *What pains He had to bear.*[7]

---

[7] Ibid.

DEATH

NUMBERS 23:10; LUKE 2:29

I once knew a fine Christian man who, as he grew older, became anxious not about death but about dying. How would he die? What would be the means of his departure from this world?

He shared these concerns with his minister, who encouraged him to take it to the Lord in prayer. Some years later, I was preaching in Morecambe when I heard that this man had passed away the previous evening. I called to see his wife and she had a wonderful story to tell.

The previous day had been their diamond wedding anniversary and the man had read the greeting cards, entertained friends and participated in a quiet family meal. At 8pm, feeling rather tired, he had gone to bed. When his wife later took him a drink, she discovered he had passed into the presence of Christ.

A wonderful end to a wonderful day, but also a wonderful answer to prayer.

DEATH OF JESUS (I)

HEBREWS 9:24-28

At school, the teacher would sometimes return work to us and because it was not up to standard, across it was written one word: REPEAT.

No such word was written at Calvary because it was a perfect work, a finished work, an unrepeatable work. And that is why God raised Jesus from the dead. God was fully satisfied with His atoning death.

DEATH OF JESUS (II)

I find it very difficult in the evening to get my wife to sit down. There are so many things that she still needs to do and because her work is not finished, she finds it hard to stop and sit down.

Again and again the Bible tells us that Jesus was received into heaven and He 'sat down at the right hand of God'. He sat down because His redeeming work was completed. It was a finished work which could never be bettered or added to.

DEATH OF JESUS (III)

1 PETER 2:24

I remember preaching with a friend outside a football ground. My friend explained how for years he had been on the side of Satan, committing every foul in the book. He then told how he had been converted. He had changed sides. He had been signed up by Jesus.

At that precise moment, a heckler in the crowd asked the very question we wanted to hear: 'How much did He give for you?'

'He gave everything,' my friend replied. 'He gave Himself upon the cross to save me from sin and death and hell.'

How true.

> *For you know that it was not with perishable things such as silver or gold that you were redeemed from the empty way of life handed down to you from your ancestors, but with the precious blood of Christ...*
>
> 1 Peter 1:18

DEATH OF JESUS (IV)

PSALM 110:3; JOHN 12:32-33; 1 JOHN 4:19

A boy and a girl were in the same class together at secondary school but the girl had no time for the boy. Indeed, she said some very derogatory things about him. And yet, some twelve years after school, this same boy and girl got married.

I was at their wedding, but I don't recall the girl being dragged screaming down the aisle against her wishes. On the contrary, when the minister asked, 'Do you have this man to be your lawful husband?' she said, 'I do.' There was no compulsion, it was her own voluntary decision. What had happened between school and this moment? The man had courted and wooed the girl, until she now wanted to be his wife.

No one ever becomes a Christian who does not want to be a Christian. No one is ever dragged against their wishes into the kingdom of heaven. No, Jesus said, 'I, when I am lifted up from the earth, will draw all people to myself.' His cross draws reluctant sinners to Himself. Jesus makes men and women willing, because they are drawn by His love for them.

DISCIPLESHIP

MARK 8:34

A young couple with two young children were wonderfully converted from the world. They had no Christian background but thrived on the Word and made real spiritual progress.

One Sunday, twelve months after their conversion, they were not at church either morning or evening. This was most unusual, so after the evening service I drove to their home. Here I was met by two disheartened believers who were facing family problems and pressures at work. The man looked me in the eye and said, 'I never knew it would be like this.'

If he never knew, it was not the fault of Jesus, because again and again He stressed the hardships and pressures of discipleship. Jesus never 'pulled the wool over anyone's eyes'. He told it as it was.

Perhaps sometimes we are almost dishonest in our presentation of the gospel because we are seeking converts and not disciples.

ETERNITY

2 CORINTHIANS 4:18; MARK 8:36-37

Salt Ayre Tip is a household waste recycling centre on the outskirts of Lancaster and Morecambe. Whenever I visit it, I am reminded that 'the things which are seen are temporary' (2 Corinthians 4:18, NKJV), because ready for disposal are fridges, washing machines, cookers, dishwashers, televisions, computers, etc. Once they were prized and cherished but now they are broken, rusted and rejected.

A few days before my grandfather died at the age of eighty-eight, he handed his pocket watch to my uncle saying, 'Take this – I won't be needing it anymore.' He recognised that, for him, time was ending and eternity was beginning.

How important that we distinguish between the things which are temporal and the things which are spiritual. Or, as Jesus put it, 'What good is it for someone to gain the whole world, yet forfeit their soul? Or what can anyone give in exchange for their soul?'

EVANGELISM (I)

MATTHEW 28:18-20

My mother always fed the birds and it is a tradition that I have happily continued. One day, when my two-year-old grandchild, Saul, was staying with us, we went out to feed the birds together.

We both had a piece of bread in our hands and, breaking my bread into small pieces, I put it on the bird table. I then turned round to see what Saul was doing and there he was – eating the bread himself.

Sometimes as believers and as churches we keep the gospel to ourselves, whereas Christ commands us to share it with others. In the words of Vince Havner:

> 'Too many Christians are stuffing themselves with Gospel blessings while millions have never had a taste.'

EVANGELISM (II)

1 CORINTHIANS 3:6-7

As a boy, I had my own patch in the garden. I am told that on one occasion I sowed some seed and the very next day I was turning the soil over to see if the seed was growing. However, that was none of my business. My task was to sow and to provide the right conditions; it was God's business to bring forth the fruit.

It is the same in the work of evangelism. We sow the seed, and we water it with our prayers – but only God can produce the harvest.

EVANGELISM (III)

1 CORINTHIANS 15:58

As enthusiastic young converts, we set ourselves the task of placing a gospel tract into every home in Morecambe. It was a colossal undertaking, but armed with street maps, we ventured out with zeal and gusto.

Every Monday evening, winter and summer, rain or shine, we took to the streets and eventually the task was completed. We perhaps thought we would convert the town and were a little downcast when the response was negligible. However, we had done what our Master had commanded us to do. We had attempted to share the gospel with the inhabitants of our town and we could leave the outcome in His hands.

EVANGELISM (IV)

LUKE 5:27-31

A short time ago we had to buy a new kettle. I am not sure how long we'd had the old one but I do know that it wore itself out in the work of evangelism. I cannot begin to calculate how many cups of tea and coffee it brewed, as Pat offered drinks to people in our home. In the end, it could take no more; hence our need for the new one. But it had indeed been the Lord's kettle.

As soon as Matthew (Levi) was converted, he invited people into his home, and we must never underestimate the importance of that kind of bridge building. O for more kettles to burn out for the Lord!

EVANGELISM (V)

MATTHEW 18:6; 2 CORINTHIANS 6:3; COLOSSIANS 3:5-6

In the 1980s and 1990s, upwards of forty children attended our weekly children's meeting. It was a privilege to spend time with them and to teach them Bible stories.

There was, however, a downside. When the school or Cubs or Brownies were having a sponsored walk, then a stream of children made their way to our home. They wanted 'Uncle' John and 'Aunty' Pat to sponsor them. We could have said no, we could have sent them away, but we never did. Why? We did not want to put any hindrance or obstacle in their way. We did not want to cause any unnecessary offence and so we were prepared to tolerate the inconvenience and the financial expense.

Paul said:

> Be wise in the way you act towards outsiders; make the most of every opportunity. Let your conversation be always full of grace, seasoned with salt, so that you may know how to answer everyone.
>
> Colossians 4:5-7

Whether witnessing to children or adults, our 'walk' is just as important as our 'talk'.

EXAMPLE (I)

1 TIMOTHY 4:12

In the 1970s, many a Saturday afternoon in September and October was spent witnessing on the promenade at Blackpool. It was the time of the illuminations, and crowds flocked to the resort every weekend. At times it felt almost as though one was witnessing in Sodom and Gomorrah but nonetheless never a weekend passed by without some profitable conversations.

One afternoon I got talking to a young man who was not hostile; on the contrary, he seemed to agree with what was being said to him. I was hoping that I was challenging him, but he then said something which challenged me.

'I am on the outside of the church,' he said, 'because my father is on the inside.'

Apparently his father was a well-known lay preacher but he was so ashamed of how his dad treated his mother and children, he had vowed never to go to church again.

I have no reason to doubt the truth of what he was saying, but what a challenge to all pastors, preachers and professing Christians. Am I one thing in church on a Sunday and something altogether different the rest of the week? Having trusted Christ as my Saviour, am I now following Him as my example?

EXAMPLE (II)

1 PETER 2:21

My headmaster at Morecambe Grammar School had a saying which he repeated over and over again, especially when sports teams were travelling to take part in competitions: 'Wherever you go, you take the good name of Morecambe Grammar School with you.'

As believers, wherever we go, we take the good Name of Jesus Christ with us, and to some extent what people think of Him will be determined by what they see in us. The example I set – is it a help or a hindrance? Are people more likely or less likely to be drawn to Christ because of me?

EXAMPLE (III)

A young couple had been wonderfully converted from the world and the change in them was most dramatic. But one Saturday they went out with their two young children for the day and it was one of those occasions when everything went wrong.

It was a hot day, the trains were late and the children were arguing and bickering. Suddenly – tired and frustrated by the day's events – the father swore at his boy.

'Daddy,' his son responded, 'I didn't think you used that word now that you know Jesus.'

The father was rebuked and humbled, and there are times when we all need to be rebuked and humbled, especially if we are putting obstacles in the way of children and young people.

FEAR

PROVERBS 29:25; MATTHEW 10:28

When I was a paper boy, I was bitten by a corgi and on another occasion by a Jack Russell. This had an effect on me and I have always been wary, even scared, of dogs. And yet, there have been times when I have shown no fear.

For example, when my children were young, if we met a dog, I would say, 'It won't hurt you. It won't bite you. There is nothing to be afraid of.' What had happened? My fear of dogs had been superseded by a greater fear; the fear of transferring my feelings to my children, or perhaps the fear of appearing to be a wimp in front of my children. One fear had been superseded by another.

> *The fear of man brings a snare.*
> Proverbs 29:25 (NKJV)

We can almost be paralysed by fear when faced by men and women... What will they say? How will they react if they know I am a Christian? Perhaps better to lay low, say nothing and retain my friendship with them. There is only one antidote to the 'fear of man' and that is a true and healthy 'fear of God'.

'Fear Him, ye saints, and you will then have nothing else to fear,' says the old hymn[8]. May such a fear override every other fear.

---

[8] Through All The Changing Scenes of Life

FAITH

LUKE 16:19-31

For several years in the 1970s, I went down to Wembley Stadium on Cup Final Day, not to watch the match, but to take part with others in open air witness.

1976 was a memorable year because Southampton, the underdogs, were playing Manchester United, the hot favourites. Southampton were known as 'The Saints' and Manchester United as 'The Red Devils', and down Wembley Way there were many banners saying that the 'Saints' were going to beat the 'Sinners', or that the 'Red Devils' were going to beat the 'Saints'.

This gave us good openings as open air preachers, and we were able to engage in conversation with many of the supporters. I talked with a Southampton supporter who said, 'I will be a believer if Southampton win – but I don't think it will happen.' Well, to the shock of the football world, it did happen – Southampton won by one goal to nil. But I would be very surprised if the result brought that Southampton supporter to repentance and faith. In the excitement and joy of the occasion, I expect he forgot the promise he had made.

Faith comes by what we hear and not by what we see.

GIVING (I)

1 CORINTHIANS 16:2-3

In Methodism, there were officers in the church known as 'poor stewards'. As a boy, I used to think that either they had no money or they were not very good at their jobs. Of course, it did not mean either of those things. At the Communion Service there was always an offering for the poor and these were the men who administered that fund.

In remembering the One who 'though he was rich, yet for your sake he became poor' (2 Corinthians 8:9), how appropriate it is to express our thankfulness by being generous to others.

GIVING (II)

MATTHEW 6:1-4

For a number of years, a few days before Christmas, an envelope would be put through our door containing a generous monetary gift. To this day, I do not know who sent the gift but I do know how, as a pastor with two young children, that gift was welcomed and appreciated.

According to the Sermon on the Mount, Jesus loves not only a cheerful giver but also an anonymous giver.

GLORIFICATION

1 JOHN 3:2

In the 1970s, I handed the 'dole' out to an unknown, unemployed, penniless young woman. Not many years later, she was a famous comedy actress with her own shows on the stage and television. What a transformation!

However, it pales into insignificance when we consider the transformation awaiting the child of God. Now we are unknown, despised, even persecuted, but when Jesus comes again we will be glorified and we will shine as the sun in the kingdom of our Father.

GOODNESS AND MERCY

PSALM 23:6

My brother came up from Wigan to take our ladies' meeting in Ingleton and, as his custom was, he arrived in good time for a meal. That evening also happened to be the night of our annual children's party, and Pat had been busy all morning making sandwiches, buns, biscuits, etc. When it was time for the ladies' meeting, Pat put the food in the boot of Jim's car, as it was a means of getting them down to the church.

Jim took the meeting, stayed behind for a drink and then shot off to Wigan with all the food still in the boot of his car. I got a frantic phone call from Pat and I set off in hot pursuit. After seven or eight miles, I saw Jim's car in the distance and, with headlights flashing, I raced up behind him.

Now, when Jim saw this speeding car with its headlights flashing, perhaps he thought, 'Oh no, an unmarked police car – what speed was I doing when I went through that village?' Of course, it wasn't a police car at all, it was me and I was on an errand of mercy. I was there to save the children's party and to save my brother the embarrassment of arriving in Wigan with a boot full of food.

Sometimes it does seem that we are being pursued by trials and troubles, but at the end of the journey the believer will be able to testify with David that he has not been

75

pursued by trials and troubles, he has instead been followed by the goodness and mercy of his God.

GOSPEL (I)

LUKE 23:23-25

For a time, in the Department of Employment, it was one of my responsibilities to try to obtain work for released prisoners. This was never easy, as many employers were understandably apprehensive about those who had served a prison sentence.

In preaching the gospel, we are asking men and women to trust One who was arrested, tried, found guilty and sentenced. How wonderful that millions have indeed come to trust in Him.

GOSPEL (II)

1 PETER 1:18-19

When Aaron came to us as a ten-week-old baby, we were told that he had been baptised with water from the River Jordan. Whatever we might think about infant baptism, the vital thing is not the water gathered from the Jordan but the blood shed on Calvary.

GOSPEL (III)

JUDE 3

Many years ago I was talking to the principal of a ministerial training college. He told me that Abraham had to find a message for his generation, Jesus for His generation, Paul for his generation, and so on. Therefore, we had to find a message for our generation.

What a tragic comment. We have no need to find any new message for this or any other generation; we must instead preach the same gospel that Jesus entrusted to his disciples, once and for all time.

GOSPEL (IV)

ISAIAH 64:6; ISAIAH 61:10

Pat received an invitation to a Royal Garden Party at Buckingham Palace and she graciously asked me to accompany her. Weeks were spent in dress shop after dress shop, looking for that special outfit. Eventually she found what she was wanting, and very nice it looked too. So much time had been spent concentrating on Pat's outfit that I mistakenly thought I had passed 'under the radar' – but I hadn't.

One Sunday morning, just a few weeks before the special day, I said to Pat, 'I think this suit will do for the garden party.'

I immediately knew I had said the wrong thing. A look of disgust came over her and she almost snapped, 'You are not going to the Palace dressed like that.'

What I thought was good enough was, apparently, not good enough for the Queen, and within days I was choosing not just a new suit but all the accessories as well.

People think that they can appear before God just as they are, but the Bible says no.

All our righteous acts are like filthy rags.
Isaiah 64:6

We each need that new suit which God Himself provides when we come to faith in His Son.

GOSPEL (V)

REVELATION 7:13-17

People are invited to the Royal Garden Party because of who they are and what they have achieved. And so, on our visit, we were mixing with mayors, ambassadors, politicians, bishops – with those who had made a valuable contribution to their communities. They were appearing in the presence of the Queen because of what they had done.

How different it will be in heaven. Not one of us will be there because of what we have done – we will only be there because of what Jesus has done. Only through His sacrificial death will we be worthy to appear in the presence of God.

GOSPEL (VI)

TITUS 3:4-5

I don't mind admitting it, but I am the world's worst when it comes to DIY. One day I was knocking a nail into a wall in the hall, but by the time I had finished the wall in the hall had almost been replaced by a hole in the wall. I am lethal with a hammer and it has always been a disappointment to Pat that my DIY skills are *nil*.

However, there is one area of DIY where we all fail and that is DIY salvation. How many feel that by their works and efforts they can make themselves acceptable to God, but they can't? We are all dependent on the perfect, finished work of Christ for our salvation.

Gospel (VII)

John 10:9; John 14:6

One afternoon I had to take my wife and Aaron for an overnight stay at Manchester Children's Hospital. I drove to Manchester, left them at the hospital and then made my way back to Ingleton.

As I drew up outside my house, I began to feel my pockets for the house key. No key could be found in my pockets or in the van. I checked our 'secret location' in the garden, but still no key. I tried the front door and the back door without success and, as the windows were all shut, access through an open window was not an option.

I decided to telephone Pat at the hospital but as it was in the days before mobile phones, I had to walk to the local telephone kiosk. Eventually I got through to the ward and I said to Pat, 'The house key, do you know where it is?'

There was an ominous silence and then Pat said, 'Oh, I don't know what I was thinking of. I locked the door and then I put the key through the letter box.'

I forget what my reply was but I am sure it was very gracious! I returned to my house, not quite knowing what my next step would be.

A short time earlier, we had had an extension built at the back of the house and so I applied some pressure to the bathroom and bedroom windows. There was no movement. But I then pressed against a window in the conservatory and it moved, and with even more pressure it came open. But my problem was not yet solved, as the window was several feet off the ground. Hoping that no one was watching, I placed a wheelie bin under the window, clambered on to the sill, fought my way through a jungle of plants and eventually landed inside the house. And there, behind the door, was the key.

That day there was a back window into my house but there is no back door or back window into heaven. There is only one door and that door is Jesus. He said:

> *'I am the door. If anyone enters by Me, he will be saved...'*
>
> John 10:9 (NKJV)

How many are trying a back door – seeking to be good, helping other people, going to church? All commendable things, but of themselves they will never get us into heaven. There is only one way to heaven and Jesus is that Way, only one door and Jesus is that Door.

GOSPEL (VIII)

MATTHEW 7:13-14; LUKE 14:15-24; 2 CORINTHIANS 6:2

In the 1970s, I regularly went to Blackpool when the illuminations were on, to engage in open air evangelism. One of my favourite venues was the Brunswick Working Men's Club, where, with others, I used to preach as vast numbers queued, waiting for the doors to open. Every week there were those who failed to gain admittance: some because they did not have the right documentation, but others because as they got towards the front of the queue, a steward would raise the sign 'CLUB FULL'.

Universalism teaches that everyone will get to heaven, but that is contrary to what Jesus taught. We need the correct documentation because 'small is the gate and narrow the road that leads to life, and only a few find it'. We need to have repented of sin and trusted Jesus as Saviour, because only those who have done so will gain entrance to heaven.

That is the solemn truth, but the good news is – heaven is not yet full. When Jesus comes again it will be, but until He returns there is still room. How vital it is that we do not delay in making our commitment to Christ, for we never know when the day of grace will end and the Day of Judgement begin.

GOSPEL (IX)

TITUS 3:4-7; HEBREWS 10:12-14

My father was quite a heavy smoker, as were many men of his generation. He often had sweets in his pocket, but there would also be bits of tobacco there. I knew this because whenever he handed me sweets during a Sunday service, amongst the sweets there would be traces of tobacco. There was evidence of his smoking even in the sweets he offered to me.

Sadly, because we are sinners, something similar is true of everything we offer to God. Whether it be our money or our good works, all that we offer to God is tainted and spoiled by sin. That is why we need to rest and trust in the only sacrifice that was perfect and without sin, the offering of Jesus upon the cross.

GUIDANCE

PROVERBS 11:14

In 1976, as a lay preacher, I took a service one August Sunday evening at Ingleton Evangelical Church. Unknown to me, there were two experienced pastors in the congregation.

As we shook hands at the end of the service, one of them put his hand on my shoulder and said, 'I think you should be in the ministry.' Even though this had never been said to me before, I gave it little thought until some three years later. It was then that I had a visit from two elders asking me to prayerfully consider the pastorate of their church. The elders were from... Ingleton Evangelical Church.

Coincidence? I do not think so. God guides principally through His Word, but also through our circumstances and the counsel of godly people.

HEAVEN (I)

JOHN 14:2-3

I am a twin, but I was born in the days before scans and consequently my mother never knew that she was having me. She knew she was having my brother, but what a surprise when forty-five minutes later I appeared! I was not expected, but I still came to a home which had been prepared because I had the warmth, the love and the care of my mother.

How much more is heaven 'a prepared place for a prepared people'? There are many things about heaven that we don't know, but believers have the assurance of the Saviour's love and presence.

HEAVEN (II)

MATTHEW 17:1-4

The week my twin brother was married, his wedding photograph appeared in the local paper. A few days later I was in Morecambe town centre when a man rushed up to me, shook me by the hand and said, 'Warmest congratulations! I have just seen your photo in the paper.' I had no desire to embarrass the poor man and so I just thanked him and made a hasty exit.

There will be no errors of identification in heaven for as Moses, Elijah and Peter recognised one another on the Mount of Transfiguration, so believers will recognise one another in heaven. What is imperfect now will be perfect then.

HEAVEN (III)

JOHN 17:24

It is five years since my mother died, but I still call at her house to see my brother. The garden is the same, much of the furniture is the same, and yet it is not the same house. It is not the same house because Mother is not there. And that is the reason I used to call; not to see the garden or the furniture, but to spend time with her. Mother was the attraction of the house.

The same will be true of heaven. There will be many things that will thrill us but the real attraction will not be the pearly gates or the jasper walls. No, the real attraction will be Jesus. 'Where I am' was the description of heaven given by Jesus. And it is the best description of all.

HEAVEN (IV)

1 CORINTHIANS 6:9-11

For many years I was a paper boy, and I remember that my first wage was the princely sum of 12s 6d. Up at six, out in all weathers, it was a job which I greatly enjoyed. Christmas was always a special time, as appreciative customers were most generous with their seasonal tips and I could often buy all my presents with the extra money I received.

One memory of having a paper round was seeing a familiar sign on many a porch window: 'No Hawkers. No Circulars. No Trespassers.' A sign is already posted on the porch of heaven: 'No Thieves. No Adulterers. No Drunkards. No Unrepentant Sinners.' How vital that we are washed, sanctified and justified before we leave this earth and enter eternity.

HEAVEN (V)

1 CORINTHIANS 6:9-11

A highly esteemed believer had been called home, and the next day I preached on heaven, emphasising what our brother was now enjoying.

After the service, a ninety-year-old man asked, with a twinkle in his eye, 'Is envy a sin?'

At first, I was rather taken aback, until I recognised just what he was saying:

> *I desire to depart and be with Christ, which is better by far...*
>
> Philippians 1:23

HEAVEN (VI)

HEBREWS 13:14

When I worked in the Department of Employment, some claimants were registered as 'NFA' – no fixed address. If they were fortunate, they would perhaps have a few days in a hostel, followed by a few days in bed and breakfast accommodation. If they were not so fortunate, it might be sleeping on a park bench or on the sand under the pier. They were NFA.

As believers, we are pilgrims in this world – we have no permanent address. But we are not NFA because we are citizens of heaven. Our permanent home is in the city of God.

> *Here in the body pent,*
> *Absent from Him I roam,*
> *Yet nightly pitch my moving tent,*
> *A day's march nearer home.*[9]

---

[9] From the hymn 'For Ever With The Lord' by James Montgomery

HEAVEN (VII)

JOHN 14:2-3

I am not very domesticated. I am spoiled, always having had a mother or a wife to cook my meals. Therefore, it is to my shame that if I was to prepare a meal for you, then my advice would have to be, 'Don't eat it.' Whereas, if my wife was to prepare a meal for you, then my advice would be, 'Do eat it!' How good, how excellent the meal is – it is largely determined by who has prepared it.

That is how we know that heaven will be perfect. It has been prepared by Jesus – the Perfect One, the Sinless One. Prepared by Jesus who in six days made the heavens and the earth. No wonder David said:

'You will fill me with joy in your presence, with eternal pleasures at your right hand.'

Psalm 16:11

Heaven (VIII)

2 Corinthians 5:6-8

My brother, after four major operations, had been in hospital or nursing homes for sixteen months. As he gained strength, we discussed his accommodation options for the future and there seemed to be four alternatives: he could return to his own home, downsize and buy something smaller, go into sheltered accommodation or remain in a nursing home. He was undecided but then he suddenly had a relapse and died shortly afterwards.

Ken was a believer and I now see there was a fifth and better option. The Lord called him to his heavenly home – a home incomparably better than any we can ever experience on earth; a home where the believer enjoys the immediate presence of Jesus.

HOLY SPIRIT

JOHN 14:26; JOHN 16:13

Jehovah's Witnesses and others deny the personality of the Holy Spirit. They teach that the Holy Spirit is a force, a power, not a Person.

I once asked a Jehovah's Witness how the Holy Spirit could be a Comforter if He was not a Person.

His answer was quite ingenious: 'A hot water bottle can comfort you and that is not a person.'

'That may be true,' I responded, 'but can a hot water bottle teach you? Can a hot water bottle guide you into all truth?' Here the analogy obviously fell down, because it is clear from the Scriptures that the Holy Spirit is a Person. He is the third Person of the Trinity, the third Person of the Godhead.

HYPOCRISY (I)

MATTHEW 2:7-8, 6:2,5,16, 7:20-23; ACTS 8:9-24

It was five o'clock on a Friday evening when I opened the door to a middle-aged man who was distraught and crying. I invited him in and my wife made him a cup of tea.

What a tragic tale he had to tell. He had come from France to commence a three-week course which started at Lancaster University on the Monday. A month earlier, his wife had died. As a result, he had gone to pieces and failed to sort out his finances. A cheque was waiting for him at the bank on Monday morning, but he had no money, no food and no accommodation for the weekend.

'Can we take it to the Lord?' he asked, and then he prayed with passion. Having prayed, he then asked, 'What time are your services on Sunday? I must meet with the Lord's people.'

To say I 'smelt a rat' is an understatement, but it has always been my policy to give such people the benefit of the doubt, in case I was 'entertaining an angel unawares'. Consequently, we provided him with a meal and I gave him money to spend the night at the Youth Hostel. I arranged to meet him the next morning but was not surprised to hear he had not spent the night at the hostel. As he walked through the village, he had got into conversation with two believers who had insisted he spent the night with them.

By now, the rat was not just 'smelling', it was 'stinking', and I told the man that I had given him all the help that I felt I could give. He thanked me profusely and said he would see me at the service in the morning. Surprise, surprise, he did not turn up at the service, and months later I discovered from the police that the 'crying conman' was wanted for offences throughout the country.

We would not descend to such levels of deceit, dishonesty and hypocrisy, and yet there is a warning. Jesus reserved His most severe words for those who pretended to be His followers but their hearts were far from Him. I may be able to preach, pray, prophesy, speak in tongues and yet still be a hypocrite. King Herod asked the wise men where he could worship Jesus. The Pharisees prayed, fasted and gave alms. Simon the sorcerer was baptised. They were not sincere or genuine – they were all hypocrites.

Lord, save me from hypocrisy, from self-deceit, from pretending to be something I am not.

HYPOCRISY (II)

MATTHEW 5:23-24; JAMES 3:10

I had travelled seventy miles to take the services at an evangelical church. Throughout the day, I was conscious of tensions in the church but I was not prepared for what happened after the evening service. We had remembered the Lord's death at His table, but within minutes of announcing the benediction, voices were being raised and I could hear the deacons arguing in the vestry. What hypocrisy! A sad end to a difficult day.

Jesus said that we need to be reconciled to one another before we come to the table, or it would be better if we never came at all. And James succinctly tells us, 'My brothers and sisters, this should not be.'

INTERCESSION (I)

MARK 6:45-52; HEBREWS 4:14-16

In the Department of Employment, I worked with a fraud investigator who was collecting evidence on those who were working yet claiming benefits. He sat in his car reading a newspaper, but he had cut out two squares in the paper so that he could see the man who was painting, building or cleaning windows. To the casual passer-by he appeared to be just reading his paper, but his eyes were constantly on those who were defrauding the public purse.

In heaven, Jesus is praying to His Father but His eye is still upon His followers on earth. We are never abandoned or forsaken. He has promised that we will never be tried beyond what we are able to bear. And so He watches, knowing how much we can and cannot endure.

INTERCESSION (II)

HEBREWS 2:17-18; HEBREWS 4:15

I met Paul when our son Aaron was in hospital. He was training to be a physiotherapist. Some months later, I saw him on a ward and enquired how he was doing.

'Fine,' he said, 'but I have just had time off with a bad back.'

'That is not good for a physio,' I joked.

'Oh it is,' he responded, 'I can now sympathise with my patients!'

As the writer to the Hebrews said, 'We do not have a high priest who is unable to feel sympathy for our weaknesses.'

> Saviour, breathe forgiveness o'er us.
> All our weakness, Thou dost know.
> Thou didst tread this earth before us.
> Thou didst feel its keenest woe.
> Lone and dreary, faint and weary,
> Through the desert Thou didst go.[10]

---

[10] From the hymn 'Lead Us, Heavenly Father, Lead Us' by James Edmeston

101

JUDGEMENT (I)

ROMANS 3:19

Having been involved in a minor road accident, I was asked to take a breathalyser test. The strange thing was that even though I am teetotal, I felt guilty and almost expected the test to be positive.

I felt guilty when I had no cause to be. How will sinners feel when they stand at the judgement seat of Christ, knowing that they are guilty?

JUDGEMENT (II)

JOHN 5:22; 2 TIMOTHY 4:8

For several years I was the umpire for Ingleton Cricket Club. I always tried to be fair and scrupulous, but undoubtedly there were times when I made wrong decisions. Indeed, if anything, in trying to be fair and neutral, I was perhaps even biased towards Ingleton's opponents! It's not easy being an umpire or referee, as anyone who has officiated at matches will testify.

It is annoying and frustrating when an umpire or referee gets a decision wrong, but football and cricket are only games. It's far more important that judgements are right when it comes to eternal issues – determining whether our destiny is heaven or hell.

Thank God, these judgements are not in the hands of mortal men, but in the hands of the Lord Jesus Christ. He is the God/Man and therefore, at the Great Assizes, Jesus will not be biased towards God nor biased towards man. His judgement will be fair and honest and scrupulous. The Apostle Paul calls Him 'the righteous Judge'. He will get it right.

JUDGEMENT (III)

NUMBERS 32:23; MATTHEW 12:36; ROMANS 14:10-12

Pat's parents visited Australia and brought a boomerang back for our son, Andrew. We went out into the fields to try it out, but only ever had a modicum of success.

Boomerangs do not always come back, but sin does. Sometimes it happens in this life – hence the saying, 'What goes around comes around.' But if not in this life, then certainly in the life to come. 'Be sure your sin will find you out' is a stern Bible warning. How vital to know that all our sins have been forgiven in Jesus.

KINGDOM OF HEAVEN

HEBREWS 12:25-29

Many of us will have sermons which stand out in our memories. I remember Dr Martyn Lloyd-Jones preaching at the Ashton Hall in Lancaster in 1978. He spoke on the topic 'we are receiving a kingdom which cannot be moved'. In a masterly way, he showed how temporary and transient were all the kingdoms and empires of this world, and that the only enduring, indestructible kingdom was the Kingdom of God.

I came out of the meeting on that June evening, marvelling at what it meant to be a Christian. I was a citizen of heaven, a member of the one kingdom that can never be moved.

LAW

ROMANS 3:23

Twice in one week I was reprimanded for speeding. On both occasions I was caught doing thirty-five miles per hour in a thirty miles per hour area. I am sure others had been caught doing forty or fifty miles per hour, but their speed did not make me any less culpable. I had broken the law and had to face the consequences.

People are always keen to compare themselves to other people because it makes them feel good about themselves. The standard, however, is not other people, it is the Law of God; and if we are honest, we all have to confess that we have fallen short of that standard.

LOVE FOR CHRIST

EXODUS 21:5; 1 JOHN 4:19

When we lived in Morecambe, we often saw people walking their dogs on the beach. One dog had been on a lead until it got to the beach, but then it was unleashed and the dog was given its freedom. Now, with that kind of freedom, the dog could have bolted off and never have been seen again. But that never happened. The dog would run ahead – sometimes a good distance ahead – but it always returned to the side of its owner. Why? Though it was not bound by a lead, it was bound by something even stronger – a love, a devotion to its owner.

As the followers of Jesus, we are not bound to Him by a contract but by something far deeper. We are bound by a love, a devotion, and though at times we might wander, again and again we return to His side.

And round my heart still closely twine
Those ties which naught can sever,
For I am His, and He is mine,
For ever and for ever.[11]

---

[11] From the hymn 'I've Found A Friend' by James Grindlay Small

NAME OF JESUS

MATTHEW 1:18,23; LUKE 2:21

At junior school, one of the boys in my class was called Chester. He had been given this name because this was the town in which his parents had met. He must have been thankful that they had not met in Giggleswick or Ashby de la Zouch!

Names are given to children for a whole variety of reasons. When we fostered children, we never had to decide what to call the baby boy or girl because they always came to us already named.

The same was true for Mary and Joseph... 'They shall call His name Immanuel – God with us' ... 'You shall call His name Jesus – He will save his people from their sins.'

Jesus came already named – and what a wonderful name! It tells us who Jesus is and what he came to do.

NEW AGE

ROMANS 5:1

A friend in the Midlands telephoned to tell me that an oak tree opposite his home had been knocked down to make way for a new housing estate. He was sad to see the tree destroyed, and yet there was something which made him even sadder...

A group of residents attached a cross to the tree and on it wrote the age of the tree, the date it was knocked down and the words 'rest in peace'. Later, at a Harvest Thanksgiving Service, a local church invited neighbours to 'come and mourn for the oak tree and make your peace with nature'.

That is New Age teaching – not the gospel. The gospel invites us not to make our peace with nature but rather, through the death of Jesus, to make our peace with God.

NEW BIRTH (I)

2 CORINTHIANS 5:17

Just days after I had been converted to Christ, I had tickets to see the American singer Solomon King. I was very much into '60s pop music and I had bought Solomon King's hit record 'She Wears My Ring'.

I went, as arranged, with a friend to where the singer was performing, but before he came on to the stage a so-called comedian was the warm-up act. He subjected us to a barrage of 'blue' jokes and after a few minutes I said to my friend, 'I am not listening to this.' And so I walked out and never did hear Solomon King.

I might have been disappointed to miss the pop singer but afterwards I was encouraged by the realisation that this was evidence that I was a 'new creature in Christ'. Weeks before, I might have disapprovingly listened to the comedian but not now – I was walking in newness of life.

NEW BIRTH (II)

ROMANS 6:4

We met Mr Moxham when we had been on honeymoon in Llandudno, and we continued to receive Christmas cards until we moved to Ingleton in 1979. Then the cards stopped and we presumed that, as he was an elderly man, Mr Moxham must have died.

In 1982, I was working in my study, when walking past the window was... Mr Moxham. Pat had gone to visit a friend but I immediately telephoned her, as I thought it might be too much of a shock to see a 'dead' man walking. Later that day we met up with Mr Moxham and it transpired that he knew we had moved to Ingleton but he had mislaid our address.

Dead men don't walk, and so if a person has a desire for worship, for prayer, for Bible study, that is a sure sign that they have been raised from spiritual death and have found new life in Christ. Dead men don't walk, and that is why we all need to experience the new birth.

New Birth (III)

1 Peter 1:23

A fine Christian man who had been brought up in a Christian home, and always attended church and Sunday School, had come to faith in Christ as a young man.

One day, he confided to me that he almost wished that he had been a thief or a drunkard before conversion, and then the change would have been more dramatic. I knew what he meant, but I asked him to consider the multitudes brought up in Christian homes, nurtured in church and Sunday School, and yet today are as far from God as they could possibly be. In every case, the new birth is a testimony to the amazing grace of God.

New Heaven and New Earth (I)

Psalm 8:6-8

My fellow elder, Ken, and I both had a fear of dogs, so we were not always the best partnership when it came to door-to-door visitation!

My fear originated from my days as a paper boy when I had twice been bitten – once by a dog that strolled up to me, wagging its tail, before sinking its teeth into my ankle.

I realise that most dogs are friendly and harmless. Indeed, one day, knocking on a door, Ken and I met a dog and the owner assured us that it could talk. She called for it and sure enough the dog barked 'hello' – with a pronounced canine accent!

There will be no fear of dogs or spiders or any animal in the new heaven and the new earth. Paradise will have been restored and man will again have dominion over the beasts of the field, the birds of the air and the fish of the sea.

NEW HEAVEN AND NEW EARTH (II)

ROMANS 8:19-22; 2 PETER 3:13

In a Shropshire town centre, a young man tried to get me to become a member of Greenpeace. It turned out to be a wonderful evangelistic opportunity, as the man confided that his neighbour was a Christian doctor, for whom he had the utmost respect.

He listened carefully as I explained to him that whilst Greenpeace might have good motives for wanting to save the planet, ultimately the planet is not waiting for Greenpeace to do something; it is rather waiting for Christ to do something. It is waiting for the day of His return, when the heavens and earth will be dissolved and Jesus will usher in a new heaven and a new earth, in which righteousness will dwell.

He still tried to sign me up for Greenpeace, but I trust I had given him food for thought.

Old Age

1 Corinthians 2:9; 2 Timothy 4:6-8

I was once chatting to an elderly neighbour who was telling me about his schooldays and his war experiences. During the course of our conversation he made this sad comment: 'Forgive me, John, for always talking about the past, but when you get to my age, you don't have a future.'

How different it is for elderly saints. They know that the best is yet to be. They have a glorious future, a wonderful hope, because they know that their future and their hope are centred in Christ.

OMNISCIENCE (I)

PSALM 139:1

In the 1950s my uncle had one of the first tape recorders and he hid it at a Christmas family party. Later that evening, he played it back and my grandma said, 'That's not me. I never said that.' But it was her. She had said that. All her words had been recorded.

How sobering to realise that all our thoughts, words and deeds have been recorded by God; that nothing is hidden from His all-seeing eye.

> *Everything is uncovered and laid bare before the*
> *eyes of him to whom we must give account.*
> Hebrews 4:13

Thankfully, He wipes the tape clean if we turn to Him in repentance and receive His forgiveness (Isaiah 43:25).

OMNISCIENCE (II)

JEREMIAH 17:9; PSALM 139

A doctor friend told me it is not always easy to discern if a bad back is genuine or whether it is being used as an excuse to take time off work.

On one occasion, he had signed a man off work for a fortnight, only later to see the man in a pair of overalls and with a ladder on his shoulder. It appears the man wanted time off work in order to paint his house.

Our excuses can be similar to a bad back. Others cannot always discern whether they are real or whether they are phoney. But God can. He knows whether 'I was too tired' or 'I was too busy' or 'I could not afford it' was the truth or just a selfish excuse.

Pastors and Teachers

(I)

Petrol stations are now few and far between, especially in rural areas. This has meant that on several journeys I have travelled anxiously as the petrol gauge has registered empty. Two or three times I have been caught out, but more times than not I have been surprised by how far my car could run on empty.

The same can be sadly true of pastors, teachers and Christian workers. We are not close to the Lord, we are not filled with His Spirit and yet we can sometimes continue ministering for months without people knowing that we are 'running on empty'. However, we know and the Lord knows. Therefore, how vital it is to wait on Him and to each day seek that fresh infilling of His Spirit.

PASTORS AND TEACHERS

(II)

MATTHEW 7:15-23; MATTHEW 24:23-25;
2 CORINTHIANS 4:2

After years of having vehicles which ran on petrol, I purchased a van which ran on diesel. One August morning, I put fuel in the van and we had a most enjoyable ride to Hexham in Northumberland.

Having parked the van, we had lunch and an enjoyable afternoon in the town, but when we wanted to return to Ingleton the vehicle would not start. I telephoned the RAC, but whilst I waited for them to come I realised what had happened. Yes – I had put petrol not diesel in the tank, and in so doing I had potentially done damage to the engine.

It is a sobering thought, but Jesus said that teachers can travel far on the wrong fuel. Many have been deceived, and before Christ returns many more will be deceived by false teachers and false prophets. They have impressive, successful CVs, but their ministry has been self-centred not Christ-centred. They have not 'rightly divided the word of truth' but have 'handled it deceitfully'.

One day, it will be revealed that they have been running on the wrong fuel, but in the meantime what potential damage have they done to the souls of men and women? We need to always be on our guard against false teachers.

PENTECOST (I)

ACTS 2:1-12; PSALM 85:6; HABAKKUK 3:2

I was born on 17th November 1947, and that date was so significant that it was recorded on a certificate – a certificate which I still have in my possession. An unrepeatable day, the day of my birth. Since then, I have had birthdays and some of them have been special; for example, my 21st, my 40th, and my 65th birthday, when I received cards – some of them cheeky – as well as gifts and presents. These were special, memorable days, but not days that can ever be compared to the day of my birth.

Pentecost was the day when the New Testament Church was born. An unrepeatable day, when things happened which might never happen again. People from every nation under heaven heard the Apostles speak in a language they could understand. This was the day the Early Church was born; a day which can never be repeated.

But since then, the Church has had her birthdays – special times when there has been a fresh outpouring of the Spirit and the Church has been revived and sinners converted. Not a repetition of Pentecost, but a perpetuation of Pentecost. And in the dark days in which we live, how the Church in Britain needs another birthday!

PENTECOST (II)

PSALM 80:18B-19

It was a calm autumnal afternoon as I walked by the River Greta in Ingleton. The river was slow and tranquil, with twigs and sticks floating on the surface of the water. The next day, I did the same walk – but now, what a difference! The river had become a torrent and was gushing by, taking logs and branches with it.

What had happened? Overnight, there had been heavy rain and it had made all the difference to the river.

Today, the Spirit of God is at work in Britain, otherwise no one at all would be converted. The Spirit is present, but often gospel work is slow and nothing much seems to be happening. How we need Pentecostal showers! How we need seasons of refreshing from the presence of the Lord to turn the stream into a torrent. Only then will sin be washed away and multitudes swept into the kingdom of heaven.

PRAYER (I)

LUKE 11:5-10

One Saturday night, just before midnight, we were wakened by a persistent knocking at our front door. I went downstairs and asked, 'Who is there?' 'You don't know me,' was the response, 'but I am an evangelical.'

I opened the door and there before me was a tramp wanting something to eat and a bed for the night. Pat made him a snack and I then took him down to the church where I made him comfortable for the night. The following morning he had a cooked breakfast, he came to the morning service, and after a roast lunch he went on his way with a couple of pounds in his pocket.

He was a man in urgent need and the need was so great that he did not hesitate to get me out of bed at midnight. I think he would have been a Methodist, a Baptist or an Anglican – depending at whose door he was knocking.

Nevertheless, he was not ashamed to make his need known and to plead for help. In the parable of 'The Friend at Midnight' did Jesus not advocate a similar response?

PRAYER (II)

ACTS 12:12

We had an elderly widower staying with us on holiday for a week, and on the Tuesday evening at 7.30pm, he asked to be excused and went to his bedroom. Tuesday at 7.30pm was the time of the prayer meeting back at his home church in London and he wished to join with them at the Throne of Grace.

Would not our churches be stronger if more believers had the attitude of that elderly man? How few attend the prayer meeting when they are at home, never mind thinking about it when they are away on holiday!

PRAYER (III)

PSALM 95:6

One of my earliest childhood memories is of visiting my grandparents' home. When it was time to leave, Grandad would commend us all to God in prayer. Grandad was an elderly man but we all followed his example, as he got up from his chair and on to his knees. Posture is not the most important thing in prayer but I learned as a child that speaking to God was different from speaking to anyone else.

PRAYER (IV)

ROMANS 12:12; COLOSSIANS 4:2;
1 THESSALONIANS 5:17

When our daughter, Joanna, was at university, we arranged for her to have a telephone installed in her student accommodation. The phone was installed on 21st September but when she got her first bill, she was being charged for calls that had been made from the 7th September – a fortnight before the phone had been installed.

It fell to Dad to try and sort out the problem. Thankfully, at that time you could still speak to a BT supervisor, and over a period of several weeks I spoke to a very helpful man. Indeed, I developed quite a relationship with him. We were on first name terms and we chatted about our wives, our children, our work and many other things as well. The relationship developed because the problem was not resolved right away.

We might think how wonderful it would be if every request was granted, every situation resolved, and every need met the first time we brought it to the Lord in prayer. But *would* it be wonderful? I suspect not, because it would mean that little time was spent in His presence. We would make the request and not think about the One to whom we were praying.

No, because prayer is not always immediately answered, it necessitates that we go to the Lord again and again. We do spend time in His presence, and as we do so, our relationship with Christ grows and develops.

PRAYER (V)

ISAIAH 49:8; LUKE1:5-7,11-13

My grandfather died at the age of eighty-eight, and six months later, at the age of twenty-one, I was converted. Grandad never saw my conversion. Does that mean the prayers he offered for me over the years were a waste of breath? Not at all. Our prayers are filed in heaven and at the acceptable time, God takes down the file and answers our prayer.

An angel said to Zacharias[12], 'Your prayer has been heard. Your wife Elizabeth will bear you a son...' As 'Elizabeth was not able to conceive, and they were both very old', this prayer had perhaps been offered many years before. But now, in heaven, God was taking down the file and the prayer was being answered.

Believer, pray on! We never know when that heartfelt request will be answered, but it will always be at a time acceptable to God.

---

[12] or Zechariah (NIV)

PRAYER (VI)

ACTS 12:11-12

In the days when most homes had coal fires, wood was needed as well as coal. Chopping sticks was almost a hobby to my grandfather and often when we called on him, he would be in his hut, surrounded by wood. On one occasion, however, he was not chopping sticks, he was doing something equally important: he was sharpening his axe. How necessary this was, if the sticks were to be chopped and ready for the fire.

It is good when a church is active, preaching and evangelising – reaching men and women, boys and girls with the gospel. Evangelical churches must be evangelistic churches, but something else is essential. How vital it is to seek the Lord and plead with Him for His blessing on our evangelistic endeavours. This is why we can never underestimate the importance of the prayer meeting. Are we trying to chop sticks with a blunt axe?

PRE-EMINENCE OF

CHRIST

COLOSSIANS 1:18

I was handed a booklet by a Jehovah's Witness. As I flicked through the pages, I remarked, 'I can't find Him – where is Jesus?' I had to keep my face straight when the man responded, 'If you turn to the index, then you will find Him.'

Surely, we should always be able to find Jesus, without having to search through the index. Jesus should never be hidden away at the bottom of page 5 or 25. He is the Incarnate God, the Great I AM. In all things, He must have the pre-eminence.

PRESENCE

EXODUS 33:14

Some years ago we had a number of friends round for an evening meal. In total, there were seven of us, but Pat had set out eight places.

As Pat apologised for the error, a man in the group made a significant comment. 'No need to apologise, Pat,' he said. 'It is a reminder that we have an Unseen Guest.'

PROCRASTINATION

HEBREWS 3:7-8A,13,15; HEBREWS 4:17

For many years, my day has begun at 7am with the Today programme on Radio Four. Jack de Manio, John Timpson, Brian Redhead, John Humphrys – some of the great names in broadcasting – have all introduced this well-loved programme.

It isn't, however, just Radio Four which has a Today programme; the Bible also has one. The time to repent of sin is *today*. The time to stop backsliding is *today*. The time to start serving Jesus is *today*.

What about tomorrow? I can only assume that tomorrow must be a most remarkable day, with more than twenty-four hours in it, because so much is going to be done tomorrow...

PROVIDENCE (I)

PHILIPPIANS 4:19

Our honeymoon was booked in North Wales but a rail strike meant we were dependent upon the kindness of a neighbour to take us to Llandudno in his car. The arrangement was that he would come back for us on the following Saturday.

However, during the course of the week, the rail strike was settled and so we would be able to come back on the train. The night before we were due to return, we went down to the railway station and, to our consternation, we discovered that we did not have sufficient money for the tickets.

That evening, in the Christian guest house, we prayed specifically for this desperate need to be met. The following morning, after breakfast, I went to settle up with the proprietor of the guest house, who greeted me with the words, 'My, you've kept that quiet. I didn't know you were on your honeymoon.' I then discovered that he had knocked a few pounds off our bill and that was sufficient for us to buy our rail tickets.

PROVIDENCE (II)

MATTHEW 6:31-34

As a pastor with a wife and two young children, money was often tight, and yet again and again we proved the goodness of God. One morning the car needed a new tyre and so off we went to Kwik Fit. As Pat and I sat in the waiting room, drinking coffee, the mechanic came with the news that we did not just need one tyre, we needed four. Our hearts sank because we knew that once we had paid for the tyres, there would be nothing in reserve.

As we travelled back to Ingleton, Pat said there was now no alternative – she would have to find a job. This was something we had never wanted, as the children were young and Pat wanted to be available to work within the church. It seemed, however, to be a case of 'needs must'.

We had lunch and that very afternoon we received a phone call from social services. A few months earlier we had been accepted as foster parents and there was now a baby requiring parental care. We gladly took in the child, and as a result of foster allowances received, there was no need for Pat to find work outside of the home.

PROVIDENCE (III)

PSALM 18:30

I started preaching in 1969 but did not have a car until 1979. This meant that for ten years I was dependent on public transport or on the kindness of relatives and friends.

One Sunday afternoon, I was due to preach in Clapham (North Yorkshire) and decided to go by train. All went well until the train developed a fault at Wennington station. Several minutes passed and then I asked the guard when he thought the train would go again. His not-too-helpful response was, 'Your guess is as good as mine.'

I made the decision to get off the train and hitchhike to Clapham. As the first car appeared, I put out my thumb and, to my surprise, the car stopped. In the car was a Christian young man whom I knew and he was on his way to see his fiancée in Ingleton. I got in the car, Desmond put his foot down and I arrived at the church in Clapham with just two minutes to spare.

PROVIDENCE (IV)

2 CORINTHIANS 12:7-10

God often helps us and provides for us in unexpected ways. But not all providences are happy; some are dark and yet even when the providence is bleak, we can still detect the good hand of our God.

As a child, whenever I had a cold or flu symptoms, my mother would bring out the Fennings Fever Mixture. The very sight of the bottle was almost sufficient to convince me that I was feeling better. It had a most bitter taste. Years later, I discovered that before I took the mixture, Mother always sweetened it with sugar to make it more palatable. What it must have tasted like without the sugar does not bear thinking about! Some providences are dark and bitter, but we can depend upon our Father in heaven to sweeten such providences with evidence of His grace and mercy.

Paul had a 'thorn in the flesh' and he found it so distressing that three times he pleaded with the Lord for it to be removed. The thorn, however, was not removed and Paul later rejoiced that it was so. Through the thorn he proved that God's grace was sufficient and that when weak, it was then that he was strong.

REPENTANCE (I)

2 CORINTHIANS 7:9-10

One Saturday night I was giving gospel tracts out in Queen Street, Morecambe, and I got into conversation with a man coming out of one of the public houses.

During the course of our conversation, he told me that in all probability he would commit adultery that night, but it did not matter because he would be at confession in the morning. I told him that God would not even hear his confession. There is true repentance but there is also false repentance.

I was out in the car listening to Gardeners' Question Time when a simple question was asked: 'How can I peel an onion without crying?' This set me thinking. The onion-peeling tears are not tears of joy nor tears of sadness – no, tears are being shed because one's eyes are smarting. What a picture of false repentance. People claim to be sorry for their sin but often they are only sorry for the consequences of their sin. They are smarting, and it is that which produces the tears and a profession of repentance.

REPENTANCE (II)

MATTHEW 3:1-2, 4:17; ACTS 2:38, 20:21; 2 PETER 3:9

Living in the country, I have never liked driving in busy city centres. When we visit our daughter in Leeds, I now insist that she drives if we are going into the city centre. What finally did it was this...

One morning, I was driving in the city, when I came across some roadworks and Joanna said, 'Dad, you will have to take the next turn left.' This I did, and ended up in an underground car park. The only way out was to turn round and come back the way I had come in, but that was not easy. I needed a ticket and so, even though I was not stopping, I had to buy one. Having bought the ticket, I was now able to go out the way I had come in.

I had gone wrong. I had to recognise I had gone wrong. Then I had to do a U-turn and go in the opposite direction to the one in which I had been going.

That is an illustration – not a perfect one – of repentance. Before I could turn round or change direction, I had to buy the ticket. And that is why it is not a perfect illustration; because, where repentance is concerned, I do not have to buy the ticket. No, the price has been paid for me. It has been paid by the death of Jesus Christ on the cross of Calvary. And so now I can repent, I can come back to God, because Jesus has done all that is necessary.

Have you turned round? Have you changed direction? Have you thanked God and trusted Jesus – who paid the price for us?

RESURRECTION (I)

ACTS 10:37-43

One Easter I met a man on a door-to-door visitation and we began to talk about the resurrection. He had no problems with the resurrection because he had the explanation: Jesus was a twin and once He had been crucified, then the other twin took over. Men must be rather desperate if they have to concoct such a story to explain away the resurrection.

How better to trust in the accounts of the gospel writers than to be influenced by the fables of men.

RESURRECTION (II)

HEBREWS 9:28A; ROMANS 4:25

Our first home in Morecambe – a pleasant three bedroom semi – was bought in 1971 for the princely sum of £3,650. By the time that we moved to Ingleton in 1979, the price of the house had quadrupled. Buying a house in Ingleton was not straightforward as, at the time, few houses were on the market and those that were for sale required the buyer to put in an offer. Our first offer was turned down, but our second offer of £12,000 was accepted and work then began on renovating and making the property fit to live in.

I came to see that an offer is only of any value if it is accepted – otherwise an offer is a worthless thing. On the cross, Christ offered Himself as a ransom for our sin, but if the offer had not been accepted by God then it would have been of no value. But – praise God! – the empty cross and the empty tomb are the proof that His sacrifice for sin was fully acceptable to God. God raised His Son from the dead and received Him back into heaven because He was satisfied with the offering for sin that Christ had made.

Resurrection (III)

John 11:23-26

It was Easter Sunday morning. The sun was shining. The church was packed. The pastor announced Charles Wesley's great hymn 'Christ the Lord is Risen Today'. The organist played the first note and then – he collapsed. Minutes later, we were told he had died.

It was an Easter Day I shall never forget because we were tangibly in the presence of death, but also in the presence of the Conqueror of death. We were shocked by the sudden home call of our brother, but our sorrow was tempered by the assurance that Jesus was risen from the dead.

Jesus said to Martha, 'I am the resurrection and the life. The one who believes in me will live, even though they die; and whoever lives by believing in me will never die. Do you believe this?'

That Easter morning, we could truly answer with Martha, 'Yes, Lord!'

SALVATION (I)

2 CORINTHIANS 5:10; ROMANS 5:6-8

It was a bitterly cold March day and I was hurrying to get our son Aaron into his specially adapted van, when in my haste, having secured Aaron's wheelchair, I carelessly locked the car keys in the vehicle. This was a potentially serious situation as Aaron is prone to fitting and must have regular medication. We thought of ringing the RAC or a local garage, but it was a Saturday afternoon and time was the essence.

Eventually I said to Pat, 'Why not ring the Fire and Rescue?' And that is what we did.

Within minutes, we heard the siren and a fire engine was with us. Four men jumped out, and when they heard of our predicament they could not have been kinder. They went to the state-of-the-art fire engine and emerged with – wait for it – a *wire coat hanger*.

For over half an hour they attempted to unlock the door, but vehicle manufacturers today are wise to potential car thieves and all their efforts came to nothing. Eventually, they broke a side window, and when the door was opened, there was Aaron smiling and none the worse for the experience. He had been rescued from a potentially serious situation.

Aaron did not realise the danger he was in. Similarly, in their sin and rebellion against God, men and women do not realise the danger they are in. Aaron, because of his multiple disabilities, was unable to do anything about his situation; and men and women are quite incapable of saving themselves. For Aaron to be rescued, it needed outside intervention, and that is true for sinful men and women too. Jesus came from heaven to earth to do for us what we could never do for ourselves. He came to die upon a cross in order to save us, to rescue us from our sins. Praise God for outside intervention!

SALVATION (II)

2 TIMOTHY 1:12

When I worked in a bank, people had deposit boxes in which they placed coins, jewellery, wills, documents, etc. – things which were precious and valuable to them.

These boxes were handed in to us and they were then kept safely in the vaults of the bank. The boxes were not left at the corner shop or the public house; they were left at the bank because they had confidence that we could keep safe what they had committed into our care.

The most precious thing any of us has is our eternal soul. The devil wants our souls, and so how vital it is that we commit them into the care and keeping of the Lord Jesus Christ. For, thank God, not only is Jesus able to save, He is also able to keep. Therefore, souls committed to Him are safe and secure for time and for eternity.

Sanctification (I)

Colossians 3:8-14

A young man attended our church who, prior to his conversion, had been a hippy. He still dressed as a hippy and had some 'way out' clothing.

Eventually, he started going out with a young lady from the church and almost immediately there was a remarkable change in his dress. He now wore a shirt and a tie. He even bought a suit. What a change! The old gear had gone and new gear had been put on. But why? He had a new affection, a new relationship, and it could be seen – even in his wardrobe.

Paul uses this very picture in Colossians 3. As believers, we have a new affection, a new relationship, and this should be seen in our spiritual wardrobe. We 'put off' those things which are grievous to the Lord and we 'put on' those graces and virtues which are pleasing to the Him.

How is your spiritual wardrobe? Are there old attitudes you need to get rid of and new things you need to put on?

SANCTIFICATION (II)

ACTS 27:23; EPHESIANS 4:1-2

After a six months probationary period in the bank, every employee went to Liverpool for an interview with the District General Manager. Nervously, having had a haircut and dressed in suit and white shirt, I went for the appointment.

The greeting from the DGM was not what I had expected. 'You need a haircut, and take that pen out of your pocket,' he said. 'We are members of a profession and we must dress accordingly.'

As believers, we are members of the Body of Christ and we must 'dress accordingly'. This applies to the clothes we wear but also to our 'spiritual wardrobe'.

Do our conversation, conduct and demeanour convey to others 'whose we are and whom we seek to serve'?

SATAN

As a pastor in a country area I often visited farms and sometimes I had to walk past sheepdogs that were tethered to a post. They barked and growled as I passed. How thankful I was that they were not free to roam! Nevertheless, I still kept a safe distance from them.

St Augustine said:

> 'The devil is like a mad dog that is chained up.
> He is powerless to harm us when we are outside
> his reach, but once we enter his circle we expose
> ourselves again to injury or harm.'

Praise God that Satan is bound – but do not underestimate the length of the chain.

SECOND COMING (I)

DEUTERONOMY 29:29; ACTS 1:7; MARK 13:32

It was 1986 when a card appeared in a shop window in Ingleton. A man had moved into the village and wished to meet with anyone who was interested in the Second Coming of Christ. I telephoned the man and arranged to call at his home one evening.

When I got there, he produced a book on the Second Coming, which he had written himself. It was quite a work, containing charts and calculations and stretching to over two hundred pages. The book reached its climax in the closing pages, where we were informed that Jesus would return in 1984. Despite already being two years out of date, the man was not at all perturbed. He explained that with the passing of time, certain calendars had changed but he was confident that he would be right to within a few years.

How foolish! Not even the angels in heaven know the time of the Lord's return. It has been hidden from them, just as it has been hidden from us. We must not, therefore, attempt to reveal what God has been pleased to conceal. Jesus said to His disciples, 'It is not for you to know the times or dates the Father has set by his own authority.'

SECOND COMING (II)

1 JOHN 2:28

As a small boy, if I was misbehaving, my mother would sometimes say to me, 'Your dad will be home soon.' I didn't know whether Dad would be home early, at his normal time or whether he would be working overtime, in which case I would have been in bed when he got home. The important thing was not the timing of his coming but rather the certainty of his coming. That was usually sufficient for me to modify my behaviour and to be the young boy I ought to have been.

It is the same with the Second Coming of Christ. The important thing is not the timing of His Coming but the certainty of His Coming. He may come today or next year or it may be in a hundred years' time, in which case we shall all be in our beds when He comes!

The fact that He is returning should cause us to walk in this world in such a way that we shall be 'unashamed before him at his coming'.

SECOND COMING (III)

1 THESSALONIANS 4:16

I visited an elderly lady and she told me how a few days earlier, she had been listening to the news on the radio, when she had fallen asleep. She had then been roused by the sound of a trumpet and in her drowsy condition she had rushed to the window, quite certain that it heralded the return of Christ!

It was nothing more than a brass band concert on the radio, but how wonderful to be ready and anticipating His return.

SECOND COMING (IV)

MATTHEW 24:36-44; ROMANS 8:19-22

Picking my children up at railway stations pinpointed two truths concerning the return of Christ. On the first occasion, on getting to the station, I checked the announcements board and it had the words I wanted to see: 'On time'. The same is true of the Second Coming. Sometimes we might feel that it has been delayed, but according to the Divine timetable, it is *on time*.

On the second occasion, the train pulled in and hundreds seemed to disembark from the carriages. I was on tiptoe, straining my neck, until I saw Andrew walking down the platform. In Romans chapter eight, Paul says that is what creation is doing; she is on tiptoe, straining her neck, looking out for the return of Christ.

Today, creation groans with earthquakes and volcanic eruptions, with floods and droughts. Creation groans as she waits for her deliverance, knowing that her ultimate redemption and restoration is not with Greenpeace or Friends of the Earth; she knows that her ultimate redemption and restoration lies in the coming again of Jesus Christ.

SECOND COMING (V)

1 THESSALONIANS 4:16-17; 2 THESSALONIANS 1:7-10

One Sunday afternoon, while I was distributing tracts on Morecambe promenade, I got into conversation with a woman who had been a Jehovah's Witness for thirty-five years. She was pleasant, not at all aggressive, and I ended our conversation by urging her to put on one side all Watchtower material and to read what the Bible had to say about the Second Coming of Christ.

Some eighteen months later this woman sought me out, and what a joy it was to discover she was now a true believer and had severed all connections with the JWs. As she had read 1 and 2 Thessalonians, she had come to see that the Second Coming of Christ was a visible, audible event which had still to take place. It wasn't some secret event which had already taken place, as was taught by the JWs.

SECOND COMING (VI)

MATTHEW 25:31-33

Politics has been a lifelong interest and therefore, whilst many people dread it, I enjoy a general election campaign. However, on the morning after the election, I have known very different emotions. If the party I voted for has won, I feel elated, but if they have lost, I feel a sense of dismay. The general election brings with it different emotions, depending whether you are on the winning or the losing side.

So it will be with the Second Coming of Christ. There will be two sides to the same day. For the saved – the winners – it will be a day of unspeakable joy, but for the unsaved – the losers – it will be a day of unimaginable despair. This day, this event, will bring with it widely different emotions. How vital that we are among the saved when Jesus comes again.

SECOND COMING (VII)

1 THESSALONIANS 4:16-17

I have recently been contacted by an old school friend, whom I have not seen for almost fifty years. He had gone to considerable lengths to find me, eventually sending an e-mail to the secretary of a church where he thought I might have been preaching.

Why the desire to contact me? Well, in eighteen months' time, a reunion is being held for all who took 'A' levels at Morecambe Grammar School in 1965. What a fascinating, nostalgic reunion that will be. I expect we will have to wear name tabs, otherwise we might not recognise one another.

There is, however, for believers, a reunion which will far surpass any reunion on earth. It will be 'in the air', when Jesus returns and the saints on earth are reunited with the saints from heaven; when the church militant will come together with the church triumphant. What a reunion, what a meeting that will be!

SECOND COMING (VIII)

ACTS 16:31; ACTS 17:30-31

In the late 1960s, when I worked in a bank, the doors always shut promptly at 3pm. If the doorbell rang at 3.05pm, there was always a panic amongst the staff. It meant that the bank inspectors were in town and immediately they would set about checking what money was in the tills and in the safe. If anyone had been dishonest, there was no opportunity to put things right – the inspectors had come.

On one inspection, one of the inspectors was a man I did not know but many in the bank did. Before being promoted, he had worked in that particular branch. He was the same man, but his role was now different. He was not there to help or assist, as he might have done before, but to inspect and pass judgement on what the staff had done.

When Jesus comes again, He will be the same Jesus but His role will be different. He came the first time to save – He comes a second time to judge. Today, we stand between His first and second comings, so how vital it is that we trust Jesus as Saviour before we face Him as our Judge.

SECURITY

ISAIAH 41:13; JOHN 10:28-29

When I walk with my grandson through a field, he holds my hand. But when we are walking by the side of a busy road, then I hold his hand. How reassuring it is to know that it is not me holding the Lord's hand, it is rather the Lord holding mine.

My wife is an experienced back seat driver... 'You are going too fast. You are too near the car in front. I wish you would slow down.' There is, however, some advice I do need to take to heart: 'I wish you would keep both hands on the wheel.'

Jesus reassures us in John 10 that as believers we are in His hands and also in the hands of His Father. Both hands are upon us and therein is our security.

SELF

LUKE 5:8; LUKE 18:13; ROMANS 7:24-25

An acquaintance of mine went on a 'voyage of self-discovery' and when he returned, several weeks later, he seemed refreshed and was encouraged by the many positive things which he had learned about himself. These voyages are becoming more and more popular, as people travel to India, Thailand and many other places, in order to 'find themselves'.

I, too, have been on a voyage of discovery. It did not take me to India or to Thailand; it took me to the Bible. And what I discovered about myself was far from flattering or encouraging. I discovered that in the sight of God, I was sinful, selfish and rebellious and I desperately needed a saviour. A humbling experience but a necessary one; it brought me to Jesus.

SIN (I)

It was an idyllic spring morning as I walked the Ingleton Waterfalls with my five-year-old grandson. Thousands visit Ingleton every year to see the spectacular waterfalls and to enjoy the woodland scenery.

The sun was shining, the birds were singing and the only other sound was the rushing of the water. We chatted together and Saul held my hand; grandfather and grandson enjoying each other's company. When we needed a rest, we sat on a seat and were refreshed by the snack which Pat had sent with us.

We continued our walk, but after a few minutes a hillside proved too tempting for Saul and, leaving me, he ran downhill, accelerating by the moment. The inevitable happened and Saul fell, grazing his arm and his chest. There were tears, plasters were required, and the second half of the walk was not as idyllic. He moaned and groaned, became increasingly tired and frequently told me how painful his arm was. And all this – because of a fall.

In the Garden of Eden, in idyllic surroundings, Adam enjoyed communion with God. This was Paradise. This was heaven on earth. But then Adam fell and everything changed. Sin came into the world and fellowship with God was broken. Adam became estranged from his Maker, and Paradise became 'a vale of tears' – all because of a fall.

SIN (II)

GENESIS 3:8-11; LUKE 19:10

One warm summer evening after school, my friends and I began to play cricket outside a bachelor school master's house. He went for his train at seven in the morning and did not return until six in the evening. All was going well until a wayward shot sent the ball over the wall and broke his window.

We stopped playing cricket and amused ourselves with hopscotch or other such games that occupied youngsters in the 1950s. But at 6pm, there in the distance, turning into the street, was Mr R. – the schoolmaster. What happened next? Well, we scarpered. You could not see us for dust. And why? Because we had no desire to meet the man whose window we had broken.

In Genesis 3, Adam and Eve hide from God for the very same reason. They have no desire to face the One whose commandment they have broken. It is not God who hides from men and women; it is rather men and women who, because of their sin and disobedience, hide from God. That is why Jesus had to come into the world to 'to seek and to save the lost'.

Sin (III)

Romans 9:29

As a youth, many happy hours were spent on the fairground at Morecambe. The ghost train, the helter-skelter, the bumper cars – they all had their attractions, whilst indoors there was the hall of mirrors. I always found these fascinating, because in the mirror I was either very tall and thin or very small and fat. It was me, but I was distorted.

Man is made in the image of God, but because of sin, we have a distorted image. Something of God is to be seen in mankind, but man is not what God originally intended him to be. That is why we need to be converted, to be changed so that we might be conformed to the image of God's Son.

SIN (IV)

PROVERBS 28:13

In the Jobcentre I interviewed a man who had not worked for a number of years, a man who was apparently making no effort to find work.

As we talked, he said he had a confession to make. It was this: he did not really want a job because that meant there would then be a job for someone who did. Not quite the logic one expects when a man is in receipt of welfare benefits. I think he was basically lazy, and yet he was making a vice into a philanthropic virtue.

How often we try to excuse our sin or put a gloss on it, but God is not deceived. 'All things are naked and open to the eyes of Him with whom we have to do.'

SIN (V)

Early one morning, as I walked through the fields, I was caught in a snowstorm and within minutes I was surrounded by sheep. They thought I was the farmer but I wasn't, and though in my pocket I had a packet of Werthers Originals, I had nothing with which to feed them.

The Bible says we have 'strayed like a lost sheep', and how often men and women go to places and people who can never meet the deepest needs of their hearts.

SIN (VI)

PSALM 14:1; MATTHEW 9:12-13

On door-to-door visitation one meets a great variety of people. I spent one and a half hours with an atheist, but what puzzled me was why an atheist should be so angry with a God who does not exist. I don't get angry with Father Christmas. On another occasion, I spent a few minutes with an elderly woman who was a regular churchgoer. When I told her that we were all sinners, I almost had to revive her on the doorstep. 'Sinners,' she said, 'are those nasty people out there.' In her eyes, she certainly was not a sinner!

Two very different people. Two very different sinners. One vehemently hostile, the other pleasant and respectable, but both demonstrating that they were in darkness and ignorance. Angry sinners and nice sinners – they all need the saving gospel of Jesus Christ.

Sin (VII)

Romans 5:12

I played cricket for the Ingleton midweek team for several seasons. At the start of the game, our captain tossed the coin with the opposing captain and if he won, he chose whether we batted or bowled. He made the decision on behalf of the team. If he said, 'Bat,' we batted, and if he said, 'Bowl,' we bowled.

In the Garden of Eden, Adam tossed the coin for all mankind. He was our representative, and in rebelling against God and siding with Satan, he took every member of the human race with him. And so his fall is my fall, his guilt is my guilt, his condemnation is my condemnation. We have each inherited from Adam a heart that is at enmity with God.

SIN (VIII)

PSALM 51:5

The brain of our adopted son, Aaron, was severely damaged when he was just a few weeks old. This means he is not able to speak and lacks capacity when it comes to understanding. Some years ago, we were staying at a cottage in Derbyshire when an elderly Christian lady said something which I have never forgotten. 'How wonderful to think,' she said, 'that Aaron has never knowingly sinned.'

It is wonderful. Too many times I have sinned and have known only too well what I was doing. Aaron has never knowingly sinned, but because of Adam's fall he is still a sinner – a sinner dependent on the grace of God and the redeeming blood of Christ.

SIN (IX)

A friend was driving in the country when he saw a pheasant in the road. He stopped his car, picked up the bird and put it in the back of his car. After a few minutes he heard a stirring, and to his shock he discovered the pheasant was not dead but stunned. Stopping the car again, he released it back into the open.

We sometimes think that we have mastered a particular sin and that, as far as we are concerned, it is now dead. How sobering to discover that the sin is not dead but still alive and active. Where sin is concerned, there is no room for complacency or confidence in self.

SIN (X)

1 JOHN 1:8-2:2

One of the joys of being a child in the 1950s was going to the circus... the big top, the master of ceremonies, the clowns, the animals. But, above all, I enjoyed the trapeze artists and the tightrope walkers. How brave they were, as they exercised their skills, way above the admiring audience.

However, most of them had a safety net, and though this did not lessen my admiration for them, it did mean that if anything went wrong there was something in place to stop them from crashing to the floor. I am sure the circus artists did not perform thinking that they could be careless as it didn't matter if they fell, that the net would always be there to save them. I am sure that was not their attitude at all. No, they were determined not to slip or fall, but *if they did* the safety net was a provision to ensure that their fall was not fatal or final.

The Christian does not want to sin. In his heart there is the determination not to sin, and yet there are times when he slips and falls into sin. How wonderful that in His grace and mercy, the Lord has made provision for such times: 'If anybody does sin, we have an advocate with the Father – Jesus Christ, the Righteous One. He is the atoning sacrifice for our sins...' 'If we confess our sins, he is faithful and just and will forgive us our sins and purify us from all unrighteousness.'

We do slip and fall into sin but because of this provision, our fall is not final or fatal. Thank God for the safety net – but let us be careful not to abuse it. The provision is not for those who want to sin but rather for those who do not want to sin.

SOUL

LUKE 15:8-10; LUKE 19:10

We were on holiday with my brother and his wife in Barmouth and as we came out of the sea, Lynda noticed that her wedding ring was missing. We combed the beach, but it worse than searching for a needle in a haystack.

But why the search? Well, if it had been a 5p or a 10p coin, we would not have bothered – but it was a wedding ring. It was something precious and of great value to the owner.

Jesus came to seek and to save the lost. Why? Because every human soul is of inestimable value. That is why Jesus came from heaven to earth. It is why he went from Bethlehem to Golgotha. He has sought and saved multitudes. Has He sought and found you?

SOVEREIGNTY OF GOD

ISAIAH 55:8-9; ROMANS 11:33-36

As a young and inexperienced pastor, I used to visit an elderly lady every Thursday afternoon. It was not something 'set in stone' but I soon came to see that it was not a good idea. One Thursday I was unable to visit her in the afternoon but decided to call after tea. It was a January evening, with snow on the ground, so I put my wellingtons on and walked to her home. I rang the doorbell and the reception I got was frostier than the night air. She had expected me in the afternoon and she was obviously upset that I had not come. She thought she knew my timetable and was disappointed when I did not adhere to it.

God is sovereign, but sometimes we think we know His timetable and so we get upset and disappointed when He does not act when and how we think He should. We have to bow to His sovereignty, recognising that 'His thoughts are not our thoughts and His ways are not our ways'. Not always easy to do, but necessary as 'we walk by faith and not by sight'.

Spiritual Depression

PSALM 42:11; PSALM 23

As my grandmother grew older, she found it increasingly difficult to get out of her chair. Many times I heard her say, 'I'm rigged.' When I moved to Ingleton, I learned this was an expression used of a sheep that had turned on its back and could not get up again. The sheep was 'rigged' or 'cast down'.

Sometimes, as believers, because of sin or circumstances, we can feel that we are on our backs and not able to get up again. We are 'rigged'. We are 'cast down'. This was David's experience. 'Why, my soul, are you downcast? Why so disturbed within me?'

How reassuring to know that as a shepherd tends a sheep that is 'rigged', so the Good Shepherd tends and comforts His sheep.

> My soul He doth restore again
> And me to walk doth make.[13]

---

[13] From the hymn 'The Lord Is My Shepherd', arr. by Francis Rous

SPIRITUAL HUNGER (I)

1 PETER 2:2

I once worked with a young woman who had anorexia nervosa. It was tragic to see her go from being an outgoing bubbly character to one who was weak and depressed.

There is such a thing as spiritual anorexia nervosa. Believers lose their appetite, they cannot stomach the Word of God, and how soon they become weak, depressed and discouraged.

Spiritual Hunger (II)

Jeremiah 15:16

Preaching at a church one Sunday evening, I saw a man in the congregation that I recognised from years ago. 'I didn't know Jack attended here,' I commented to a deacon.

'Jack attends any church whenever there is cake and biscuits!' came the reply.

Jack goes where the food is, and in the spiritual realm it's also important that we go where the food is. We need to regularly attend those churches where souls are fed through the faithful exposition of the Word of God.

STATE OF THE NATION

(I)

PROVERBS 22:6; PROVERBS 14:34

W hen I was a boy in the 1950s, there were around thirty children in the houses surrounding our home. Of those, only a couple did not go to Sunday School and they stood out. Today, those figures would be reversed.

Does it matter? Indeed it does. 'Righteousness exalts a nation', and when a generation is growing up without any knowledge of God or the Bible, how can we ever hope to be an exalted nation?

STATE OF THE NATION

(II)

2 CORINTHIANS 2:11

The first year that we were in our new house it was springtime. I weeded the vegetable plot but did nothing after that. Nonetheless, that did not mean that nothing happened. Within weeks, the vegetable plot was overrun with thorns and weeds and thistles.

'Do nothing' seems to be the motto of many when it comes to instructing children in the Christian faith. Do nothing and let them decide when they are older. But whilst we are doing nothing, Satan is busy sowing his seeds and soon our youth are overrun with the weeds of unbelief, the thorns of impurity, the thistles of rebellion. 'Do nothing' is a recipe for disaster and the effects are to be seen in our society.

STATE OF THE NATION

(III)

PSALM 144:15B

I remember accompanying a patient to see a psychiatrist who had come to the UK from Nigeria. Before the consultation, the psychiatrist prayed with us and commended us to the Lord. He then made the following sad statement:

'When I was in Nigeria I used to talk to my patients about the Lord, and knowing that this was the country of John Wesley and George Whitfield, I just presumed I would be able to do the same in Britain. But I am not allowed to.'

How tragic when a nation departs from God.

STATE OF THE NATION

(IV)

PSALM 33:12

One Sunday morning the weather forecaster, having told us it was going to be a misty, foggy morning, added, 'So do take extra care if you are driving to a car boot sale.' His words came back to me when, later that morning, I was almost late to a preaching appointment in Chorley. I was held up at a roundabout as cars queued to get into a field for a car boot sale.

An indication of the low spiritual state of the nation is when people would rather congregate at the CBS than worship at the C of E, URC or AoG.

STATE OF THE NATION

(V)

AMOS 8:11

P at and I were on holiday and we were rather dismayed at the number of redundant churches in the area. Buildings which had once sounded forth the Word of God were now warehouses, shops and homes. Our spirits were not raised when we bought a local paper and in the property section read an article entitled 'Praying for a home'. Estate agents were excited at the number of churches and chapels now on the market and boasted how, at a reasonable cost, they could be converted into 'fantastic family homes'.

I could not share their enthusiasm. When churches close, God is not worshipped, repentance is not preached, and so the moral and spiritual decline of a nation intensifies. A famine of the Word of God is not something to be celebrated but something to mourn. It is a further indication that the Lord is displeased with a nation.

STATE OF THE NATION

(VI)

ISAIAH 5:20-21

We were having a drive in the Cumbrian countryside when we came to a signpost at a T-junction. Sedbergh to the right was five miles, and Kirkby Lonsdale to the left was six miles. I immediately felt disorientated because I knew that the town of Sedbergh was to the left and the town of Kirkby Lonsdale was to the right.

On returning home, I telephoned the Highways Department and they later confirmed that the sign had been placed the wrong way round. How confusing – both for those who knew the area and especially for those who did not.

Are not the moral signposts in our nation now pointing in the wrong direction? Behaviour which the Bible condemns as evil is now considered to be good, whilst conduct which the Bible commends is now considered to be undesirable. When evil is presented as being good and good as being evil, our nation is in a desperate plight. No wonder youngsters now use the word 'wicked' to mean 'good' or 'awesome'.

Suffering of Jesus (I)

Luke 22:43; Hebrews 9:22

Going to the dentist now is not quite the traumatic experience it was when I was a boy. In those days, I always suffered twice. First, I suffered in the waiting room as I anticipated the ordeal that lay ahead. And then I suffered in the dentist's chair, as the treatment proceeded. However, what I suffered in the waiting room – though it was real – never solved my problem. My problem was only solved when I sat in the dentist's chair.

It would be blasphemous to equate Gethsemane and Calvary with a visit to the dentist. But did not Jesus suffer twice? First, He sweat drops of blood in Gethsemane, and then He shed His blood on Calvary. He suffered twice, and whilst we must not underestimate His sufferings in Gethsemane, neither must we ever forget that we have been redeemed, not by the shedding of sweat but by the shedding of blood.

SUFFERING OF JESUS (II)

MATTHEW 4:2; MARK 11:12; MATTHEW 8:20

I was preaching at a Christian conference in South Wales and was accompanied by Pat and Aaron. On arriving at the centre, there was a notice in the foyer indicating which rooms had been allocated to us. Our room was No.11 but against Aaron's name were the words 'no food / no bed'. Aaron is fed through a tube into his stomach so 'no food' was applicable, but though he spends his days in a wheelchair, he does require a bed at night. We gently pointed this out to the Centre Manager and he immediately arranged for a bed to be provided.

No such arrangement was made for Jesus. He was hungry in the wilderness, hungry at Bethany and He, for whom there was no room in the inn, had no guarantee of a bed at night. It was a life of self-denial and suffering.

TEMPTATION

HEBREWS 2:18; HEBREWS 4:15-16

I know an eighty-two-year-old man whose care for his wife, diagnosed with Alzheimers Disease, is exceptional. Day and night, 24/7, he cares for her. His GP tells him that his wife is in the best care home in the district – her own home. Such is his devotion and commitment to his wife.

When I got married, I too promised 'in sickness and in health', but I have never had to prove my commitment as that man has. Up to now, the vow I made has been largely theoretical, but his has been experiential. He has known the pain and stress that such commitment brings.

This is why Jesus had to be tempted. He could only be our Great High Priest by first experiencing what we experience. His temptation was not theoretical – it was real and demanding. 'Because he himself suffered when he was tempted, he is able to help those who are being tempted.'

TEN COMMANDMENTS

(I)

ROMANS 7:12

Our daughter had a hamster in a cage, and she regularly took it out for exercise and to clean the cage. On one particular day, the hamster saw her chance to escape and she disappeared under the floorboards. Joanna was heartbroken, and for the next forty-eight hours every effort was made to find the missing pet.

All attempts failed until there was a knock at the back door and there stood our neighbour with Henrietta in his hands.

'Do you know what this is?' he asked. 'I almost stepped on it.'

I tell you, there was great rejoicing in our household over the hamster that had been lost but was now found.

I suppose some might think that putting a hamster in a cage is very restrictive for the hamster, perhaps even cruel. The truth is, however, that within the confines of the cage, the hamster is far safer than anywhere else. Indeed, for the next few days Henrietta filled her pouches with food, lest she should go missing again. To some the Ten

Commandments seem narrow and restrictive, but God knows that it is only within those boundaries that society can be civilised, content and safe.

TEN COMMANDMENTS

(II)

EXODUS 20:7

In a local newspaper, the Lord's Name was taken in vain. I contacted the paper and was put through to the young reporter responsible for the article. I expressed my concern and disappointment, but she did not seem to realise what I was getting hot under the collar about.

How sad if a generation has grown up that is quite ignorant of the third commandment.

TEN COMMANDMENTS

(III)

EXODUS 20:12

A harassed and tearful mother was speaking to me about her daughter. 'She says she can prophesy and speak in tongues,' the mother said, 'but what she cannot do is help me with any of the housework.'

Whatever gifts a believer may or may not have, they are never an excuse for not obeying the fifth commandment.

TEN COMMANDMENTS

(IV)

ROMANS 3:19-20; GALATIANS 3:10-14,22-24

I was driving down the motorway and for many miles cars had been speeding past me. But then everyone began to slow down. Why? An accident? Road works? No – in the distance – a police car. That police car – the presence of the law – had a restraining impact on speeding motorists.

In a similar way, an understanding of the Ten Commandments acts as a restraint when men are tempted to do evil. How imperative it is that we pass on a knowledge of the commandments to future generations, otherwise our nation will continue on its downward spiral.

I spoke at a nursing home service on the Ten Commandments. In conversation afterwards, an elderly lady thanked me and said, 'Preach the Ten Commandments and there is no need to preach anything else.' A sad comment, because whilst the Commandments can restrain sin, they cannot remove sin. Indeed, the Commandments reveal our sin and our need of Jesus – the only One who ever kept them perfectly and yet, amazingly, died for those who had broken them.

TEMPTATION (I)

I once attended a meeting of Alcoholics Anonymous – I hasten to add, *as an observer* and not as a member! In that meeting, I was most challenged by the testimony of a recovering alcoholic. He explained that as a successful businessman, he and his wife had enjoyed three or four foreign holidays every year. But he testified that he had not been out of the country for three years. The reason was this: he had always been afraid of flying and so each time before he boarded a plane, he had always had a few stiff drinks. Now he dare not take the risk of touching alcohol and was not prepared to put himself in the way of temptation.

What a challenge to the believer! Are there not times when we put ourselves in the way of temptation? We go to places or we engage in activities where it is easy for Satan to 'gain an advantage over us'. It is no use praying, 'Lead us not into temptation,' if we then run right into it.

Evangelist Doug Barnett said:

> *'If you don't want the devil to tempt you with forbidden fruit, you had better keep out of his orchard.'*

TEMPTATION (II)

EPHESIANS 4:27; 1 THESSALONIANS 5:22;
1 CORINTHIANS 6:12

After a service, I got into conversation with a middle-aged lady. She told me that she was a believer but her husband wasn't, and this sometimes caused difficulties in the home. She proceeded to tell me that once a week she was now going to the home of a widower in the town, where they were praying and reading the Bible together. What she wanted to know was, 'Am I doing wrong?'

I think she knew the answer before she even asked the question. If it wasn't wrong, it wasn't wise; and if it wasn't sin, then it wasn't sensible.

Everything is permissible but 'not everything is beneficial'.

TEMPTATION (III)

GENESIS 3:6-8

Foolishly, I was placing out some tablets, when my sweet-loving two-year-old granddaughter came into the room. Her eyes sparkled and before I could intervene she had taken one. Desperate to prevent her swallowing the medication, I put my fingers in her mouth and managed to grab the tablet. Naturally, Elodie was upset and burst into tears.

As with Eve in the Garden of Eden, Satan makes sin attractive and irresistible, but how often it all ends in tears and sadness.

TIME

It had been a particularly hectic week and on the Thursday morning Pat exclaimed, 'I can't believe it is Friday already.' I had to explain, it was in fact not Friday but Thursday.

Whether time seems to drag or to race by, time is passing and all too soon time will end. How important it is that we do not squander this precious gift from God.

> *'Spend your time in nothing which you know must be repented of; in nothing on which you might not pray for the blessing of God; in nothing which you could not review with a quiet conscience on your dying bed.'*
>
> Richard Baxter

TRUTH

JOHN 14:2,6

When our children were young and money was tight, we saw an advert in the paper: *'Kids travel free on the train.'* Eagerly we saved the necessary coupons and looked forward to 'the train taking the strain'.

Unfortunately the offer was not quite what it seemed, as it transpired that you could not use a Family Railcard or book cheap day returns with it. The result was we ended up saving nothing. It is obviously wise to always read the small print, whether you take out insurance, open a bank account, enter a competition or collect coupons.

With Jesus, there is no small print. He not only speaks the Truth, He *is* the Truth. We can fully rest on everything that Jesus ever said.

WORK (I)

COLOSSIANS 3:22-24

Once, as a boy, I attended a testimony meeting when the Cliff College Trekkers were in Morecambe. I do not think I was paying too much attention, until a man got to his feet and said, 'I am a dustman for Jesus.' Some days later, I saw this man outside my house, taking a tea break with his workmates. They were reading the Daily Mirror; he was reading his New Testament.

A false distinction is sometimes made between Christian work and secular work. Paul made no distinction, telling the slaves in Colossae that they were serving the Lord Jesus. They were working for an earthly master but first and foremost they were serving Jesus.

> *A servant with this clause*
> *Makes drudgery divine:*
> *Who sweeps a room, as for Thy laws,*
> *Makes that and the action fine.*[14]

---

[14] From the hymn 'Teach Me, My God and King' by George Herbert

WORK (II)

DANIEL 6:3-4

I had only been working in the bank for a few weeks when a celebration was held to mark forty years of service by the chief cashier. His words to me on the morning of the meal were not very encouraging. 'Forty wasted years... Forty wasted years...' That was how he summarised his time in the bank.

It is true that some jobs are more interesting and rewarding than others, but for the believer the work years have never been wasted; not if we have worked conscientiously, always seeking to commend Jesus by our conversation and our conduct.

The task Thy wisdom hath assigned
O let me cheerfully fulfil;
In all my works Thy presence find,
And prove Thy good and perfect will.[15]

---

[15] From the hymn 'Forth in Thy Name, O Lord' by Charles Wesley

WORLDLINESS (I)

MATTHEW 6:33

A missionary friend returned home on furlough after four years in Africa. His home church kindly took him out for a meal, but he confessed he was shocked by the tone of much of their conversation. The bigger house, the new car, the expensive holiday... these things dominated their thinking.

Having ministered amongst poor believers in Africa, he questioned whether British Christians had got their priorities right.

WORLDLINESS (II)

1 CORINTHIANS 7:29-31

Pat and I had only been courting a short time when she invited me to her home for a meal. Expecting a light meal, I had already eaten a substantial amount before going to Pat's home. To my embarrassment, I soon discovered that 'tea' was, in fact, a three course meal. Needing to create a good impression with my future mother-in-law, I did full justice to the meal and ate all that was put in front of me.

That same evening, we had been invited to the home of a retired couple in the church. My stomach felt 'heavy', but even more uncomfortable when the lady of the house brought in the supper. Sausage rolls, sandwiches, scones, cakes and biscuits were set before us, and knowing the trouble the lady had taken, I felt I just had to eat.

Later that evening, I walked Pat home, gave her a goodnight kiss, and then rushed round the corner to be as sick as a dog.

Food is good and enjoyable to eat but the danger comes – as I found that night – when you abuse it. I suffered because of my over-indulgence.

There are many things in this world which can bring us pleasure. Work, art, music, sport and hobbies are all things we can rightly enjoy. The danger comes when we over-indulge and abuse these things. There are believers who are weak and sickly because work or a hobby has become an idol, and spiritual exercises have been pushed out. We are in the world but how important it is that we *use* the world and do not abuse it.

WORSHIP (I)

REVELATION 7:15

My mother-in-law attended a Baptist church and one Sunday morning the lady sat next to her said, 'You don't come at night as well, do you?' My mother-in-law said that she did, to which the woman replied, 'I only come in the morning. It's like a dose of medicine. I like to get it over with.'

The worship of Almighty God is the greatest activity that anyone can ever engage in. How sobering the words of A.W. Tozer:

> *'I can safely say, on the authority of all that is revealed in the Word of God, that any man or woman on this earth who is bored and turned off by worship, is not ready for heaven.'*

WORSHIP (II)

HEBREWS 10:25

A young man started to worship at the church but his attendance was very intermittent. One Sunday, I commented that we had not seen him for a while.

'That's right,' he said, 'some Sundays the Spirit tells me to worship God, not in church but out on the hills.'

What a blessing, I thought, that the Spirit does not tell the pastor, the preacher, the Sunday school teacher and the organist all to do the same, otherwise there would be no church at all.

WORSHIP (III)

PSALM 89:7

A pet service was advertised outside a church in Derbyshire, but this was a pet service with a difference. If you did not have an actual pet, you were invited to bring a teddy bear or some other cuddly animal and they, too, would receive a blessing.

A pastor recalled to me how he had been out on door-to-door visitation and had got into conversation with a middle-aged woman, who told him that she was now attending a church down the road. The pastor enquired what she was making of the services, to which she replied, 'They are great. In fact, they are not much different to the Working Men's Club on a Saturday night.'

It is easy to be critical, but what has the church in Britain come to when we are blessing teddy bears and when the worship of the Godhead can be equated with the WMC?

WORSHIP (IV)

ACTS 20:7-12; ACTS 10:33

Mister R. was the organist of the church that I attended as a boy. During the sermon, he would step down off the organ, sit with his wife in the choir stalls and immediately go to sleep. As the sermon drew to a close, his wife would prod him in the ribs and he would wake 'refreshed' for the closing hymn.

In my imagination, I used to picture the congregation singing the final hymn, unaccompanied, with Mr R. still asleep!

Sometimes 'sleeping in church' is excusable if a person has a medical condition or, for example, has come off an overnight shift, but otherwise it is an insult to God and is also potentially dangerous. The gospel is being faithfully preached but needy sinners do not hear it because they are asleep.

In Acts 20, when Eutychus fell asleep as Paul preached, there was a temporary consequence. But for sleeping sinners, there can be eternal consequences. Let us not insult Almighty God and do possible harm to our souls by using worship as an excuse to catch up on our sleep.

WORSHIP (V)

COLOSSIANS 3:16

Pat has a friend who telephones her from time to time, and I always know when this particular friend is on the phone. Pat sits in her chair, and for most of the time she is silent. This, for Pat, is rather unusual, but she is quiet because she cannot get a word in. It is her friend who is doing all the talking. The phone call is not a dialogue but a monologue. It is not a conversation because there is no balance between speaking and listening.

Worship is a dialogue between God and man. Therefore it is not good if three-quarters of a service is given over to music and singing but only a quarter to the reading and teaching of God's Word. This means that man is doing too much speaking and God is not being given time to speak through His Word. There must be the proper balance. And whilst man speaking to God and God speaking to man are both important, surely it is more important that we listen to God than that God listens to us.

Contact the Author

To contact the author, please write to:

John Mollitt,
Westgate,
Croft Road,
Ingleton,
Carnforth,
Lancs.
LA6 3BZ

Or send an email to:

john.mollitt@btinternet.com